DATE DUE

INTRODUCING
ISSUES WITH
OPPOSING
VIEWPOINTS®

School
Policies

Noël Merino, *Book Editor*

GREENHAVEN PRESS
A part of Gale, Cengage Learning

GALE
CENGAGE Learning™

Detroit • New York • San Francisco • New Haven, Conn • Waterville, Maine • London

Christine Nasso, *Publisher*
Elizabeth Des Chenes, *Managing Editor*

For more information, contact:
Greenhaven Press
27500 Drake Rd.
Farmington Hills, MI 48331-3535
Or you can visit our Internet site at gale.cengage.com

For product information and technology assistance, contact us at

Gale Customer Support, 1-800-877-4253
For permission to use material from this text or product, submit all requests online at www.cengage.com/permissions

Further permissions questions can be e-mailed to permissionrequest@cengage.com

Articles in Greenhaven Press anthologies are often edited for length to meet page requirements. In addition, original titles of these works are changed to clearly present the main thesis and to explicitly indicate the author's opinion. Every effort is made to ensure that Greenhaven Press accurately reflects the original intent of the authors. Every effort has been made to trace the owners of copyrighted material.

LIBRARY OF CONGRESS CATALOGING-IN-PUBLICATION DATA

School policies / Noël Merino, book editor.
    p. cm. -- (Introducing issues with opposing viewpoints)
Includes bibliographical references and index.
ISBN 978-0-7377-5201-4 (hardcover)
1. School management and organization--United States. 2. Students--Civil rights--United States. I. Merino, Noël.
LB3012.2.S362 2011
371.2'07--dc22

2010039239

Printed in the United States of America
2 3 4 5 6 7 15 14 13 12 11

Contents

Chapter 3: Are School Policies Aimed at Student Health Effective?

Foreword

I ndulging in a wide spectrum of ideas, beliefs, and perspectives is a critical cornerstone of democracy. After all, it is often debates over differences of opinion, such as whether to legalize abortion, how to treat prisoners, or when to enact the death penalty, that shape our society and drive it forward. Such diversity of thought is frequently regarded as the hallmark of a healthy and civilized culture. As the Reverend Clifford Schutjer of the First Congregational Church in Mansfield, Ohio, declared in a 2001 sermon, "Surrounding oneself with only like-minded people, restricting what we listen to or read only to what we find agreeable is irresponsible. Refusing to entertain doubts once we make up our minds is a subtle but deadly form of arrogance." With this advice in mind, Introducing Issues with Opposing Viewpoints books aim to open readers' minds to the critically divergent views that comprise our world's most important debates.

Introducing Issues with Opposing Viewpoints simplifies for students the enormous and often overwhelming mass of material now available via print and electronic media. Collected in every volume is an array of opinions that captures the essence of a particular controversy or topic. Introducing Issues with Opposing Viewpoints books embody the spirit of nineteenth-century journalist Charles A. Dana's axiom: "Fight for your opinions, but do not believe that they contain the whole truth, or the only truth." Absorbing such contrasting opinions teaches students to analyze the strength of an argument and compare it to its opposition. From this process readers can inform and strengthen their own opinions, or be exposed to new information that will change their minds. Introducing Issues with Opposing Viewpoints is a mosaic of different voices. The authors are statesmen, pundits, academics, journalists, corporations, and ordinary people who have felt compelled to share their experiences and ideas in a public forum. Their words have been collected from newspapers, journals, books, speeches, interviews, and the Internet, the fastest growing body of opinionated material in the world.

Introducing Issues with Opposing Viewpoints shares many of the well-known features of its critically acclaimed parent series, Opposing Viewpoints. The articles are presented in a pro/con format, allowing readers to absorb divergent perspectives side by side. Active reading questions preface each viewpoint, requiring the student to approach the material thoughtfully and carefully. Useful charts, graphs, and cartoons supplement each article. A thorough introduction provides readers with crucial background on an issue. An annotated bibliography points the reader toward articles, books, and websites that contain additional information on the topic. An appendix of organizations to contact contains a wide variety of charities, nonprofit organizations, political groups, and private enterprises that each hold a position on the issue at hand. Finally, a comprehensive index allows readers to locate content quickly and efficiently.

Introducing Issues with Opposing Viewpoints is also significantly different from Opposing Viewpoints. As the series title implies, its presentation will help introduce students to the concept of opposing viewpoints and learn to use this material to aid in critical writing and debate. The series' four-color, accessible format makes the books attractive and inviting to readers of all levels. In addition, each viewpoint has been carefully edited to maximize a reader's understanding of the content. Short but thorough viewpoints capture the essence of an argument. A substantial, thought-provoking essay question placed at the end of each viewpoint asks the student to further investigate the issues raised in the viewpoint, compare and contrast two authors' arguments, or consider how one might go about forming an opinion on the topic at hand. Each viewpoint contains sidebars that include at-a-glance information and handy statistics. A Facts About section located in the back of the book further supplies students with relevant facts and figures.

Following in the tradition of the Opposing Viewpoints series, Greenhaven Press continues to provide readers with invaluable exposure to the controversial issues that shape our world. As John Stuart Mill once wrote: "The only way in which a human being can make some approach to knowing the whole of a subject is by hearing what can be said about it by persons of every variety of opinion and studying all modes in which it can be looked at by every character of mind. No wise man ever acquired his wisdom in any mode but this." It is to this principle that Introducing Issues with Opposing Viewpoints books are dedicated.

Introduction

"The very nature of cell phones, especially with regard to their text messaging capability, permits much of that activity to be performed surreptitiously."

—Justice Angela M. Mazzarelli, *Price v. New York City Board of Education*, April 22, 2008.

Between the ages of six and eighteen, most kids spend more of their waking hours at school than anywhere else. Society has long recognized the role that schools play in raising children by allowing them to create policies, enforce rules, and administer discipline. The legal doctrine of *in loco parentis*—in the place of a parent—has been recognized by the US Supreme Court to give primary and secondary schools the legal responsibility to act as parents to the children in their care. This responsibility is not without limits, but it has been upheld in several areas. The school's right to create and enforce certain policies is, at times, in tension with the rights of parents and the rights of the students themselves. One recent issue that illustrates this tension is the question of whether schools should ban cell phones.

According to a recent survey taken by the Pew Internet & American Life Project in 2009, 75 percent of twelve- to seventeen-year-olds own cell phones. Of the students surveyed, 12 percent said that they are allowed to have their phone at school at any time, and 62 percent said that they are allowed to have their phone at school but not in class. However, 24 percent said that their school has a policy that bans cell phones on school grounds. Despite the ban at some schools, 65 percent of cell-owning teens at these schools bring their phones to school anyway, and 58 percent of them have sent a text message during class. Among teens who take phones to school, 43 percent say they text in class at least once a day or more, and 25 percent have made or received a call during class time.[1]

Responding to the increase in cell phones within schools and the associated disruptions, many local school districts have banned cell phones. The New York City public school system banned the possession of cell phones in schools beginning in September 2005. Since its inception, the school policy has been a source of much controversy. Many came out in favor of the ban, such as former New York City schoolteacher Jesse Scaccia, who stated, "I can tell you that cell phones don't belong in the classroom. A student with a cell phone is an uninterested student."[2] Many parents responded to the ban negatively. One parent of a New York student, Elizabeth Lorris Ritter, supported the ban on phones in the classroom but disagreed with extending the policy to possession on school grounds: "If my children are not allowed to keep their cell phones during the school day—off and in their backpacks or lockers—the school system is governing my parenting and my children's behavior during non-school time. The school has no such right."[3]

In response to New York City's ban on cell phones, a group of eight parents—along with a citywide parent association—filed a lawsuit seeking to overturn the ban, claiming that the ban violated their constitutional right as parents to raise their children as they see fit. Some parents see cell phones as an important way for their children to reach them, especially in the case of an emergency. One of the parents who filed the lawsuit, Carmella Price, told the *New York Times*, "This is a safety issue. It's not during school. It's before and after school."[4]

In 2007 the New York State Supreme Court ruled that the ban on cell phones was a rational way for schools to prevent phone use in the classroom. Justice Lewis Bart Stone wrote, "This court finds that whatever constitutional rights a parent may have under Supreme Court precedent to void a state law or regulation for having interfered with the parents' fundamental rights to make decisions concerning the care, custody and control of their children, such rights do not apply to the controversy here."[5] On appeal, Justice Angela M. Mazzarelli agreed that a ban on possession was a justified policy for a school to make since a mere ban on use was too difficult to police, convinced by the New York Department of Education's claim that "a ban on possession of cell phones is necessary because a ban on use is not easily enforced."[6]

This is not the first controversial school policy to make its way to the courts for allegedly violating either the parent's or the child's rights. For instance, in the US Supreme Court case of *Tinker v. Des Moines Independent Community School District* (1969), it was determined that a student's right to free expression under the First Amendment precluded schools from having policies that limited student expression that was not disruptive to school activities. In *Tinker*, students had protested the Vietnam War by wearing black armbands. Whereas this kind of expression was found to be part of a student's right to free expression, other Court decisions have ruled in favor of schools, allowing them to censor student newspapers and limit student speech at off-campus events.

The debate about school policies is likely to continue, as the desire of schools to create environments conducive to learning sometimes clashes with the desires of students and their parents. The issue of banning cell phones in schools is one of the many school policies that continue to be debated. Other controversial school policies, including those related to student expression, student safety, and student health, are explored in *Introducing Issues with Opposing Viewpoints: School Policies*.

Notes

1. Amanda Lenhart, "Teens and Mobile Phones," Pew Internet & American Life Project, April 20, 2010. www.pewinternet.org /Reports/2010/Teens-and-Mobile-Phones.aspx?r=1.
2. Jesse Scaccia, "Should Cell Phones Be Banned in Schools? Yes," *New York Times Upfront*, December 11, 2006.
3. Elizabeth Lorris Ritter, "Should Cell Phones Be Banned in Schools? No," *New York Times Upfront*, December 11, 2006.
4. Quoted in Anemona Hartocollis, "School Cellphone Ban Violates Rights of Parents, Lawsuit Says," *New York Times*, July 14, 2006. www .nytimes.com/2006/07/14/nyregion/14phones.html.
5. Lewis Bart Stone, *Price v. New York City Board of Education*, 16 Misc 3d 543, June 18, 2007. www.nycourts.gov/reporter/3dseries /2007/2007_27214.htm.
6. Angela M. Mazzarelli, *Price v. New York City Board of Education*, 51 AD3d 277, April 22, 2008. www.nycourts.gov/reporter/3dseries /2008/2008_03512.htm.

Chapter 1

Should Schools Limit Student Expression?

Students at the University of California–Los Angeles occupy the hallway outside the chancellor's office in March 2010 to protest cuts in education.

Viewpoint

1

Schools Should Be Allowed to Restrict Student Speech Off Campus

John Roberts

"The question thus becomes whether a principal may, consistent with the First Amendment, restrict student speech at a school event, when that speech is reasonably viewed as promoting illegal drug use."

In the following viewpoint John Roberts, writing for the majority in this US Supreme Court opinion, claims that the First Amendment does not protect all student speech. At issue is the speech of a student, written on a banner displayed at an off-campus school-sanctioned event. Roberts contends that given the content of the message and the fact that the event was a school event, the principal of the school did not restrict the student's right to free speech under the First Amendment by taking down the banner and reprimanding the student. Roberts is chief justice of the Supreme Court, appointed in 2005.

John Roberts, majority opinion, *Deborah Morse et al. v. Joseph Frederick,* 551 US 393, Supreme Court of the United States, June 25, 2007.

AS YOU READ, CONSIDER THE FOLLOWING QUESTIONS:
  1. What was the message on the student banner at issue in this student speech court case?
  2. According to Roberts, at least two interpretations of the words on the banner demonstrate that the sign advocated what?
  3. The author concludes that the First Amendment does not require schools to tolerate at school events student expression that does what?

On January 24, 2002, the Olympic Torch Relay passed through Juneau, Alaska, on its way to the winter games in Salt Lake City, Utah. The torchbearers were to proceed along a street in front of Juneau-Douglas High School (JDHS) while school was in session. Petitioner Deborah Morse, the school principal, decided to permit staff and students to participate in the Torch Relay as an approved social event or class trip. Students were allowed to leave class to observe the relay from either side of the street. Teachers and administrative officials monitored the students' actions.

A School Speech Case

Respondent Joseph Frederick, a JDHS senior, was late to school that day. When he arrived, he joined his friends (all but one of whom were JDHS students) across the street from the school to watch the event. Not all the students waited patiently. Some became rambunctious, throwing plastic cola bottles and snowballs and scuffling with their classmates. As the torchbearers and camera crews passed by, Frederick and his friends unfurled a 14-foot banner bearing the phrase: "BONG HiTS 4 JESUS." The large banner was easily readable by the students on the other side of the street.

Principal Morse immediately crossed the street and demanded that the banner be taken down. Everyone but Frederick complied. Morse confiscated the banner and told Frederick to report to her office, where she suspended him for 10 days. Morse later explained that she told Frederick to take the banner down because she thought it encouraged illegal drug use, in violation of established school policy. . . .

At the outset, we reject Frederick's argument that this is not a school speech case—as has every other authority to address the question. The event occurred during normal school hours. It was sanctioned by Principal Morse "as an approved social event or class trip," and the school district's rules expressly provide that pupils in "approved social events and class trips are subject to district rules for student conduct." Teachers and administrators were interspersed among the students and charged with supervising them. The high school band and cheerleaders performed. Frederick, standing among other JDHS students across the street from the school, directed his banner toward the school, making it plainly visible to most students. Under these circumstances, we agree with the superintendent that Frederick cannot "stand in the midst of his fellow students, during school hours, at a school-sanctioned activity and claim he is not at school." . . .

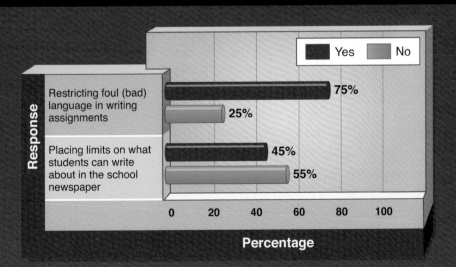

Teens' Views on Restricting Student Speech

Asked of US teens aged 13–17:
Please indicate whether or not you think each of the following steps is an appropriate measure for public schools to take.

Yes | No

Response

Restricting foul (bad) language in writing assignments
75%
25%

Placing limits on what students can write about in the school newspaper
45%
55%

0 20 40 60 80 100

Percentage

Taken from: "Gallup Youth Survey," Gallup Poll, April 15–May 22, 2005.

The Message of the Banner

The message on Frederick's banner is cryptic. It is no doubt offensive to some, perhaps amusing to others. To still others, it probably means nothing at all. Frederick himself claimed "that the words were just nonsense meant to attract television cameras." But Principal Morse thought the banner would be interpreted by those viewing it as promoting illegal drug use, and that interpretation is plainly a reasonable one.

As Morse later explained in a declaration, when she saw the sign, she thought that "the reference to a 'bong hit' would be widely understood by high school students and others as referring to smoking marijuana." She further believed that "display of the banner would be construed by students, District personnel, parents and others witnessing the display of the banner, as advocating or promoting illegal drug use"—in violation of school policy.

We agree with Morse. At least two interpretations of the words on the banner demonstrate that the sign advocated the use of illegal drugs. First, the phrase could be interpreted as an imperative: "[Take] bong hits . . ."—a message equivalent, as Morse explained in her declaration, to "smoke marijuana" or "use an illegal drug." Alternatively, the phrase could be viewed as celebrating drug use—"bong hits [are a good thing]," or "[we take] bong hits"—and we discern no meaningful distinction between celebrating illegal drug use in the midst of fellow students and outright advocacy or promotion. . . .

Student Speech and the First Amendment

The question thus becomes whether a principal may, consistent with the First Amendment, restrict student speech at a school event, when that speech is reasonably viewed as promoting illegal drug use. We hold that she may. . . .

Drawing on the principles applied in our student speech cases, we have held in the Fourth Amendment context [which guards against unreasonable search and seizure] that "while children assuredly do not 'shed their constitutional rights . . . at the schoolhouse gate,' . . . the nature of those rights is what is appropriate for children in school" [*Vernonia School Dist. 47J v. Acton* (1995)]. In particular, "the school setting requires some easing of the restrictions to which searches by public authorities are ordinarily subject" [*New Jersey v. T. L. O.* (1985)].

Former Juneau, Alaska, high school principal Deborah Morse speaks to reporters outside the US Supreme Court concerning the Court's decision to restrict student speech rights when the message seems to advocate illegal drug use.

Even more to the point, these cases also recognize that deterring drug use by schoolchildren is an "important—indeed, perhaps compelling" interest. Drug abuse can cause severe and permanent damage to the health and well-being of young people. . . .

School principals have a difficult job, and a vitally important one. When Frederick suddenly and unexpectedly unfurled his banner, Morse had to decide to act—or not act—on the spot. It was reasonable for her to conclude that the banner promoted illegal drug use—in violation of established school policy—and that failing to act would send a powerful message to the students in her charge, including Frederick, about how serious the school was about the dangers of illegal drug use. The First Amendment does not require schools to tolerate at school events student expression that contributes to those dangers.

EVALUATING THE AUTHOR'S ARGUMENTS:

In this viewpoint John Roberts contends that student speech at school events may be rightfully restricted when the content of that speech promotes drug use, but he implies that not all speech can be rightfully restricted. How does Roberts draw the line here based on the content of the speech? Do you agree with his reasoning?

Schools Should Not Be Allowed to Restrict Student Speech Off Campus

"Outside school grounds, where politics meet the streets, school regulations fade and the rules are the same as applies to citizens generally, including free speech."

Seattle Times

In the following viewpoint the *Seattle Times* argues that students should have the right to free speech off the grounds of school. Although the author agrees that certain kinds of speech may not be protected within schools, the author claims that the First Amendment protects speech outside of school. The *Seattle Times* concludes that students have the same right to free speech as other citizens when they are off school grounds. The *Seattle Times* is a daily newspaper published in Seattle, Washington.

AS YOU READ, CONSIDER THE FOLLOWING QUESTIONS:
1. According to the author, what 1969 US Supreme Court case ruled that students have a right to engage in political speech?
2. The *Seattle Times* claims that what organizations supported Joseph Frederick in his Supreme Court case?
3. What three examples does the author give of schools appropriately limiting student speech?

A case featuring an attention-seeking kid holding an absurd sign should not compel the US Supreme Court to limit free speech near high schools.

The Supreme Court and Student Speech

In 2002, 18-year-old senior Joseph Frederick stood across the street from his high school and unfurled a 14-foot banner that read "Bong Hits 4 Jesus." Frederick invoked his First Amendment right to free speech. An unamused principal, unable to maintain a cool head, ripped up the banner and suspended him, in part for using the word *bong*, interpreted as defiance of the Juneau, Alaska, school's anti-drug message. It was smart-alec behavior on the teen's part, but was it protected speech? The line between what falls within protected speech and what does not was appropriately drawn in 1969 when the Supreme Court ruled in *Tinker v. Des Moines, (Iowa)* [*Independent Community*] *School District* that students have a right to engage in political speech.

FAST FACT

In the 1969 case of *Tinker v. Des Moines Independent Community School District*, the US Supreme Court stated, "School officials do not possess absolute authority over their students."

The court should not overturn *Tinker*. But there are limits to free speech, particularly inside a school. School administrators, for example, can regulate speech on campus or at a school-sponsored event if it is vulgar, disruptive or interferes with education. An administrator of any school, public or private, needs that authority. A 1986 Supreme

Court case from Washington state, *Bethel School District v. Fraser*, sharpened the line when it upheld a school's right to restrict students from vulgar speech at a school assembly.

A Speech Case

Last week [March 19, 2007], in oral arguments before the high court, the attorney for the school district, former special prosecutor Kenneth Starr, argued that Frederick's sign glorified marijuana in defiance of the school's anti-drug massage. Justice Anthony Kennedy took issue with the provocative banner because, he said, it was not indicative of the kind of image the school wanted to portray.

If the banner had been held on campus, that would be an argument. But Frederick's banner was off campus during a non-school event, an Olympic Torch relay. The school allowed students to attend the relay but Frederick skipped school that day and went to the event on his own.

The student was in a public setting—across the street from the school but not on its grounds—and should have been free

Student members of the group Sensible Drug Policy rally outside the US Supreme Court to support Joseph Frederick's right to display his "Bong Hits 4 Jesus" banner. The Court disagreed with them.

to exercise free speech. The Court of Appeals for the 9th Circuit appropriately sided with Frederick, as have the American Civil Liberties Union and religious groups such as the Christian Legal Society, the Rutherford Institute and a law center founded by the Rev. Pat Robertson.

On the other side are anti-drug organizations and two former US drug czars. We are sympathetic to their goal of controlling drugs, but this is not a drug case. It is a speech case.

A Limit to School Authority

With children under its charge, and particularly on its property, a school needs to have a degree of authority, including over speech. That is why, for example, *The Seattle Times* opposes the bill sponsored by Rep. Dave Upthegrove, D-Des Moines, to give editorial control of high-school newspapers to the students.

Another example of schools' rights, approved by the Ninth Circuit Court after the [1999] Columbine [high school] shootings, is the expanded schools' ability to sanction students for "scary" speech, even when it has no direct impact on the school. Gun-free and

US Supreme Court Justices' Views in the Case of *Morse v. Frederick* (2007)

View	Name of Justice
The speech of student Joseph Frederick was not protected by the First Amendment (majority opinion).	Chief Justice John Roberts Justice Antonin Scalia Justice Anthony M. Kennedy Justice Clarence Thomas Justice Samuel Alito
The speech of student Joseph Frederick should be protected by the First Amendment.	Justice John Paul Stevens Justice David Souter (retired) Justice Ruth Bader Ginsburg
The speech of student Joseph Frederick does not concern a First Amendment issue for the Supreme Court to decide.	Justice Stephen G. Breyer

[Compiled by editor.]

drug-free zones have drawn a security perimeter around schools. Appropriately so.

But somewhere comes a limit to the school's authority. Outside school grounds, where politics meet the streets, school regulations fade and the rules are the same as applies to citizens generally, including free speech. Within the schools, access to free speech—from gang clothing to graffiti to pronouncements at school ceremonies—is necessarily within the realm of controlled speech.

Modern principals and superintendents, as well as the Supreme Court justices, should understand the distinction between on and off campus, between a regulated environment and the more tolerant regime outside.

EVALUATING THE AUTHORS' ARGUMENTS:

In this viewpoint the *Seattle Times* claims that the Supreme Court case about Joseph Frederick's banner is a speech case, not a drug case. How does John Roberts, author of the previous viewpoint, claim the issue of drugs is relevant to the case?

Viewpoint

3

School Uniforms Are Harmless and Necessary

"Uniforms allow children the right to distinguish themselves by the deeds they've done, not the duds they wear."

Jeffrey Earl Warren

In the following viewpoint Jeffrey Earl Warren contends that resistance to school uniforms is not about free expression but about the desire of parents to assert their identities. Rather than restrict children in any way, Warren argues that school uniforms allow children of all backgrounds to be on equal footing in the classroom. Warren concludes that school uniforms are a valuable way to allow children to distinguish themselves by their deeds and not by their clothes. Warren writes a weekly column for the *St. Helena Star* newspaper in Napa Valley, California.

AS YOU READ, CONSIDER THE FOLLOWING QUESTIONS:
1. According to the author, Baby Boomer parents use their children as billboards to advertise what?
2. What other examples of uniforms outside of school does the author give to support the view that uniforms are important?
3. Warren worries that free dress gives kids status without what?

The ACLU [American Civil Liberties Union] is taking Redwood Middle School in Napa to court, ostensibly because a child dared to wear socks with a "Tigger" logo on them.

Most people assume this is a debate of conservatives versus liberals, or conformists versus non-conformists. Despite the arguments, chances are the kids will lose because both sides are unable to see the real problem—the parents.

Parents and School Uniforms

The dress code at a public school, or school uniform question, is not about children. It has nothing to do with the right to a child's free expression.

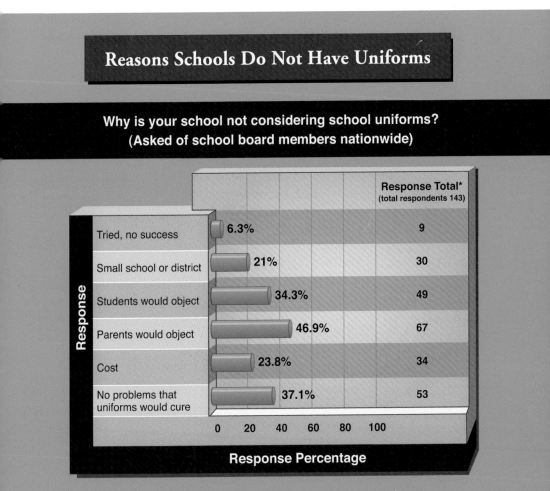

Reasons Schools Do Not Have Uniforms

Why is your school not considering school uniforms?
(Asked of school board members nationwide)

Response	Response Percentage	Response Total* (total respondents 143)
Tried, no success	6.3%	9
Small school or district	21%	30
Students would object	34.3%	49
Parents would object	46.9%	67
Cost	23.8%	34
No problems that uniforms would cure	37.1%	53

*Total is greater than the number of the respondents' answers because some respondents chose more than one selection.

Taken from: National School Board Association, 2006 NSBA School Uniform Survey.

It's about Baby Boomers [those born from the mid-1940s to the mid-1960s], who have discovered that their own children serve as excellent billboards to advertise to the world the type of parents that they are. We've had "tennis moms," "Little League dads," even Mozart mommas; that is, parents who defined their identity—and their social position—through the exposition (and often exploration) of their children's talents. But now there are an alarming number of parents who see their children the way they view Blackberrys or hybrid cars—as symbols of their position in life. That's why those who are against school uniforms make such strange political bedfellows.

It plays out this way:

"I'm rich and successful. My daughter wears only Armani."

"I'm proud to be a preppie. My boy wears wing-tips and Brooks Brothers shirts."

But it's not confined to the well-heeled. The well-endowed say, "Décolletage worked for me when I was a kid. It's plunging necklines for my daughter."

Ex-jocks join the fray. "I sired an athlete—my kid wears 49er logos to prove it."

Earth mamas, unaware that the '60s are over, show the world their beliefs by dressing their girls in loose-fitting shifts and sandals.

Rednecks announce it by decking their kids out in blue jeans and plaid shirts.

Well buffed studs encourage tight T-shirts on their boys. "World, I want you to know that I read *W* and *GQ*, so my kids are in Versace and sport the latest ponytail bob that shows you how hip I am."

"I'm a free thinker, so my kid wears whatever she damn well pleases."

"I'm cool and watch MTV, so my kid can dress like a rapper."

"I'm poor and proud of it, so my kid dresses like a slob—to hell with you rich so-and-so's."

The Purpose of Uniforms

Uniforms, or dress codes, do not restrict freedom of expression. They are neutral. They level the playing field. Rather than the "plain Jane" in the [upscale brand] Dior having an advantage over the "plain Jane" in the [department store] Mervyn's, uniforms help place kids on an equal footing. They are also a daily reminder of the social contract that all kids and parents sign—that school is different from regular life.

It matters not whether a kid is in school to sell drugs and meet babes, or trying for a scholarship to MIT [Massachusetts Institute of Technology]. Uniforms are a daily reminder that school is first and foremost a hallowed house of learning.

Uniforms remind teachers, parents and kids that an important task is at hand—if not important, at least one that is different from, say, the task when one dresses as a surfer.

Uniforms are tribal. Just as primitive man painted his face and wore outfits to honor different rituals from hunting, to war parties,

These children wear school uniforms, a policy that school administrators believe ensures that students from all backgrounds will be treated equally in the classroom.

to weddings, to religious events, we don uniforms to designate to all concerned the nature and the importance of the ritual we are involved in. We all know the code: Judges wear robes; dark suits for funerals; white dresses for weddings; shorts for weekends; whites for doctors; Sunday best for church; bonnets for Easter.

Deeds Over Duds

Uniforms are a harmless, yet necessary, form of social communication. Ever wonder why no one complains about robes for graduation? To those who are still worried about a child's right to self-expression, wouldn't it be grand if they had to express themselves via deeds, not duds?

You know: "Which one is Suzy?"

"The one with the great smile"—or "the one who won the math contest? The one who is the most loyal friend I know? The one who pitches for the softball team? The one who works at the old people's home?" There are lots of ways for kids to express themselves and stand out, short of the easy way, vis-à-vis [as compared with] simple dress.

Remember, anyone can distinguish himself via an obscene slogan on his shirt. That takes no talent. There is no merit involved—though in a teen's world, there would be status. Free dress gives kids status without merit. Uniforms allow children the right to distinguish themselves by the deeds they've done, not the duds they wear.

EVALUATING THE AUTHOR'S ARGUMENTS:

In this viewpoint Jeffrey Earl Warren argues that opposition to school uniforms has nothing to do with freedom of expression. How might a proponent of school uniforms counter Warren's argument on this point?

School Uniforms Are Ineffective and Violate Student Rights

Lee Rowland

"Uniforms are an inefficient and unnecessary bureaucracy that requires school officials to be worried about what everyone is wearing."

In the following viewpoint Lee Rowland argues that public schools should not require school uniforms for four reasons. First, Rowland claims that students have a First Amendment right to express themselves at school. Second, she argues that schools should teach the value of the First Amendment by allowing diversity of dress. Third, she contends that a student's dress is a crucial form of self-expression. And fourth, Rowland claims that school uniforms are not even effective for the goals pursued by uniform proponents. Rowland is an attorney for the American Civil Liberties Union of Nevada.

AS YOU READ, CONSIDER THE FOLLOWING QUESTIONS:
1. According to the author, students have a First Amendment right to express themselves so long as what?
2. Rowland claims that clothing is an important form of expression in school that informs an observer about what?
3. The author contends that a 1998 study from Notre Dame University found what statistically significant correlation?

Students Have Rights!

The First Amendment to the U.S. Constitution protects every individual's freedom of speech: his or her right to express artistic, religious, and political viewpoints.

In the 1970's, however, several high school students were disciplined for coming to school wearing black armbands protesting the Vietnam War. These students successfully took their free speech case all the way to the U.S. Supreme Court, which famously noted in its *Tinker* [*v. Des Moines Independent Community School District* (1969)] opinion that students "do not shed their constitutional rights at the schoolhouse gate." The Court set out a framework for dealing with students' free speech rights in school: that students have a First Amendment right to express themselves so long as that expression is not disruptive to the school day.

Disruption is the right standard—it means that students are able to express themselves so long as lessons can continue uninterrupted. Clothing is precisely the type of passive, nondisruptive medium that allows students to share their thoughts without interfering with educational opportunities. Because students' self-expression on clothing generally does not disrupt class, uniforms are an inefficient and unnecessary bureaucracy that requires school officials to be worried about what everyone is wearing. Instead, school officials should only be concerned with clothing that is actually disruptive—which both dress codes and simple common sense are more than adequate to handle.

Schools Should Teach Constitutional Values

The Constitution is so important to our daily lives that we ask public officials—and in many states, public school teachers—to take an oath to uphold the Constitution as a requirement of holding an office of public trust. Our public schools are more than just an educational necessity—they are our one shot, as a society, at inculcating the most important American values for the future citizens and leaders of our country. And perhaps no value is more crucial, and more uniquely American, than diversity of thought and expression, as reflected in that empowering first guarantee the American people saw fit to include in our Bill of Rights: the protection of the fundamental freedoms of speech, religious thought, press, or assembly.

In conflict with the First Amendment, school uniform policies create instead an environment of sterilized uniformity scrubbed of the diversity so prized by our founding fathers. Perhaps more importantly, the façade of homogeneity in no way reflects the real world that students will enter immediately upon graduation from high school.

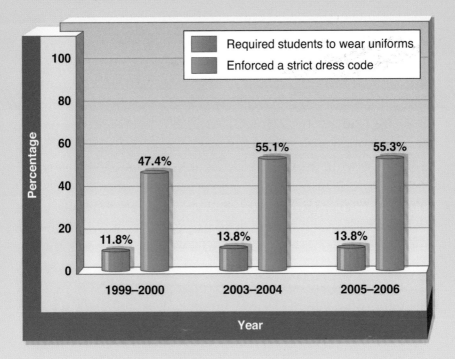

Percentage of Public Schools with a Dress Code 1999–2000, 2003–2004, 2005–2006

Taken from: Institute of Education Sciences/National Center for Education Statistics (NCES), "Indicators of School Crime and Safety: 2007," NCES 2008, December 2007.

In the real world, as in our democracy, there are conflicts of opinion in every conversation. There are messages—commercial, political, religious—shouted from every street corner and billboard. And there are beliefs and passions of every stripe. Our First Amendment encourages and protects individual expression and ensures conflict and disagreement. No one has ever said the First Amendment is easy or neat—on the contrary, it produces a glorious and legally-protected cacophony [dissonance] of ideas unthinkable in almost every other country worldwide. But the complicated nature of the First Amendment does not at all mean that we shy away from imparting its spirit to each and every student. Instead, our schools should embrace the First Amendment as a legacy of freedom that each student has the honor and duty to uphold. Forcing students to dress and look alike flies in the face of the diversity of thought and rugged individualism that are the bedrock of our nation and our Constitution.

School Uniforms Eliminate a Crucial Form of Self-Expression

Unlike a street corner, a sidewalk, or a public park, the school setting does not offer many opportunities for self-expression that do not disrupt the school day. Generally, students cannot freely post or distribute literature without school officials' permission. Sandwich boards clog the hallways, rushed conversations must end when the bell rings, and bullhorns are pretty much out of the question. Students are left with one blank canvas on which to paint their thoughts, emotions, and politics—their clothes. Whether a student chooses a religious tee-shirt, a campaign button, an all-black ensemble, or a tuxedo, he or she is sending a distinct message. Unlike a bullhorn, this message is silent and passive. Clothing subtly informs the observer who a student is, or wants to be seen as, individually.

School officials are likely to argue that school is exclusively for learning, and that self-expression is for after-school hours. But the two simply aren't mutually exclusive. In fact, the differences among student outfits are fertile grounds for identifying their likes and dislikes, figuring out if they identify as "goth" or "preppy," tracking changes in hygiene or dress that may reflect a student's psychological state, and showcasing the breadth of choice and diversity among young people. These are tools that teachers and other students can use to increase the educational experience, by getting to know students as fully-formed individuals, and talking about divergent socioeconomic and cultural norms. Furthermore, allowing students to choose their clothing is an empowering message from the schools that a student is a maturing person who is entitled to the most basic self-determination. In a freer learning environment, students begin with a sense of self-worth—rather than as identical captives without options. Giving kids a choice to express themselves not only acknowledges their individuality but creates the possibility for a relationship of mutual respect. So long as this parade of choices does not interrupt the school day, schools should be interested in nurturing, rather than standardizing, student expression.

Some people argue that school uniforms quash all means of self-expression.

School Uniforms Are Ineffective

The effectiveness of school uniforms is the subject of a raging debate, and school officials routinely claim that their own positive experiences justify the imposition of uniforms. However, such anecdotal certainty is not borne out in the largest empirical, controlled study that has been done. This 1998 study completed at Notre Dame University examined the effect of school uniforms on "attendance, disciplinary behavior problems, substance abuse, and academic achievement." The two authors, professors of sociology, debunked prior reports of uniforms' effectiveness as anecdotal. More importantly, they found that teachers' perceptions of their students once in uniform changed greatly, and that they viewed uniformed students as better-behaved, smarter, and more successful. This perception, however, was only in the minds of the teachers—statistically, the researchers found that student uniforms had no positive statistical correlation with absenteeism, drug use, attitudes toward school, or student achievement. Strikingly, the authors found only one statistically significant correlation—a negative effect on student achievement by tenth graders forced to wear uniforms.

This finding implies that some students, when forced into a standardized uniform, are negatively impacted to the point that their school work suffers. Overall, what the study shows is that while school teachers and administrators are often convinced of the effectiveness of uniforms, such an impression is the result of their own prejudices rather than actual changes in behavior. Perhaps, then, the correct solution is to work on correcting administrators' clothing-based bias, not reducing students' rights in order to compensate for the socioeconomic assumptions of the generations above them.

EVALUATING THE AUTHORS' ARGUMENTS:

In this viewpoint Lee Rowland claims that clothing is a crucial form of self-expression for students. How might Jeffrey Earl Warren, author of the previous viewpoint, argue that such expression is not important?

Schools Cannot Discriminate Against Certain Student Clubs

"The Equal Access Act serves a vital purpose in public schools by allowing many student groups to meet even though some may disagree with their ideologies, religions or politics."

David L. Hudson Jr.

In the following viewpoint David L. Hudson Jr. celebrates the federal protection of diverse student clubs, discussing the evolving application of the Equal Access Act. Hudson argues that schools must allow religious student clubs the same rights and access as nonreligious clubs. Similarly, he contends that schools must allow gay and lesbian student clubs the same opportunities as other student clubs. Hudson is a scholar at the First Amendment Center, a program of the Freedom Forum, which is a nonpartisan foundation that champions the First Amendment as a cornerstone of democracy.

AS YOU READ, CONSIDER THE FOLLOWING QUESTIONS:
1. According to Hudson, the 1984 Equal Access Act forbids schools from doing what?
2. The author contends that fourteen years after the US Supreme Court's decision in *Westside Community Board of Education v. Mergens*, the number of student Bible clubs was what?
3. What federal court case from 2003, according to Hudson, ruled that school officials cannot refuse gay-straight alliance clubs the same opportunities as other clubs?

S tudents form all sorts of clubs at school, including some not related to the curriculum. Sometimes school officials shut down such clubs because they believe them inappropriate or too controversial. For example, there is evidence that many school officials have prohibited student religious clubs because they fear that allowing such clubs would violate the establishment clause [forbidding Congress from making any law "respecting an establishment of religion"] of the First Amendment.

The Equal Access Act

In 1984, Congress passed the Equal Access Act [EAA], which forbids schools from discriminating against clubs or denying them equal access to school facilities because of their philosophical or religious viewpoints. The act was passed largely to prevent widespread discrimination against religious clubs.

Under the law if a school opens its facilities to "any noncurriculum related group," it must open its facilities to all student groups. This means that if a school allows students to form a chess club or a 4-H club, it usually must also allow the formation of a Bible club, gay-lesbian club or other group that some might consider controversial.

In 1990, the U.S. Supreme Court ruled in *Westside Community Board of Education v. Mergens* that the Equal Access Act was constitutional. In that case, the high court determined that a school district violated the Equal Access Act by denying use of its facilities to a religious club, while allowing a chess club, a scuba-diving club and other "noncurriculum-related" groups to use school facilities.

Student Bridget Mergens met with the principal at Westside High School in Omaha, Neb., to request permission to form a Christian club at her school. The principal and later the associate superintendent denied Mergens' request. They argued that having a religious club at the school would violate the establishment clause. School officials also contended that they did not have to comply with the Equal Access Act because they had not created a limited open forum. (Under the Equal Access Act, a limited open forum is created when school officials open their facilities for use by noncurriculum-related student groups. Thus, if a school allows a chess club it must also allow a Bible Club.) According to the school officials, the other student clubs were curriculum-related, rather than noncurriculum-related.

A Landmark Supreme Court Decision

The case eventually reached the Supreme Court, which ruled in favor of Mergens. The Court disagreed with the officials, and found that the clubs were all noncurriculum-related. "Congress clearly sought to prohibit schools from discriminating on the basis of the content of a student group's speech, and that obligation is the price a federally funded school must pay if it opens its facilities to noncurriculum-related student groups," the Court wrote.

The Court also rejected the school board's argument that the Equal Access Act itself violated the establishment clause. The school board had argued that the primary purpose of the Equal Access Act was religious, that the primary effect of the law was to advance religion and that it caused an excessive entanglement

> **FAST FACT**
>
> According to a 2007 survey by the Gay, Lesbian, and Straight Education Network, about a third of students nationwide have a Gay-Straight Alliance club at their school.

between religion and schools. The Court rejected all of these contentions. "Congress' avowed purpose—to prevent discrimination against religious and other types of speech—is undeniably secular," the Court wrote. "Because the Act on its face grants equal access to both secular and religious speech, we think it clear that the Act's purpose was not to endorse or disapprove of religion."

"The *Mergens* decision was a landmark ruling in the area of equal access involving student rights on public school campuses," said Jay Sekulow, chief counsel of the American Center for Law and Justice and the attorney who argued the case for Mergens before the high court. *Mergens* "upheld the constitutionality of the Equal Access Act and determined once and for all that student religious groups must be given the same access and benefits afforded to other student groups," Sekulow said. "The *Mergens* decision cleared the way for the tremendous growth of student Bible clubs on public school campuses across the nation. There were relatively few in place before the case began and now—some 14 years later—there are more than 15,000 student Bible clubs operating in school districts nationwide. The impact of *Mergens* is still felt today with the Supreme Court opinion often cited in other religious-liberties cases particularly when the rights of students are at issue."

The Ongoing Debate About Religious Clubs

The *Mergens* case did not end Equal Access Act disputes between students and school officials over the formation of student religious clubs. Punxsutawney, Pa., high school student Melissa Donovan encountered resistance at her high school when she sought permission from school officials for a Bible club to meet during the school's "activity period" between 8:15 and 8:54 A.M. each day. During this period, students could attend club meetings, go to study hall, take make-up tests or hang out in the school gymnasium. Other voluntary, noncurriculum clubs met during this time, including an anti-alcohol club and a health-services career club.

School officials argued that they did not violate the Equal Access Act because the activity period did not constitute "noninstructional time" within the meaning of the statute. Under the Equal Access Act, a school creates a limited open forum when it allows noncurriculum-related student clubs to meet on school grounds during "noninstructional time."

The 3rd U.S. Circuit Court of Appeals determined in *Donovan v. Punxsutawney Area School Board* (2003) that the activity period was "noninstructional time," writing: "Simply because the period may fall within the more general parameters of the school day does not indicate that all time within those parameters necessarily constitutes actual classroom instruction."

Religious Clubs in Public Schools

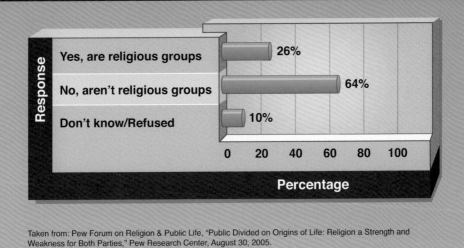

Asked of parents with children in school:

"As far as you know, are there Bible study groups, prayer groups, or other religious groups at your child's school for students to participate in, or aren't there such any groups at your child's school?"

Response

Yes, are religious groups — 26%

No, aren't religious groups — 64%

Don't know/Refused — 10%

0   20   40   60   80   100

Percentage

Taken from: Pew Forum on Religion & Public Life, "Public Divided on Origins of Life: Religion a Strength and Weakness for Both Parties," Pew Research Center, August 30, 2005.

School officials contended that the activity period should be considered instructional time because it comes after a homeroom period and the beginning of the school day. However, the 3rd Circuit emphasized that it must look more to the substance of the time period than the label placed on it by school officials. "Just as putting a 'Horse' sign around a cow's neck does not make a bovine equine, a school's decision that a free-wheeling activity period constitutes actual classroom instructional time does not make it so."

The 3rd Circuit also determined that the school's exclusion of the Bible club constituted viewpoint discrimination because the school barred it "solely because of the club's religious nature."

Attorney Lawrence G. Paladin Jr., who represented Donovan, said the decision was an important one. "The actual decision in *Donovan* is quite broad," he said. "It allows students to meet for religious and philosophical purposes on the same basis as other groups."

He added that the decision and the Equal Access Act were particularly important for student Christian clubs. "In our culture we are turning more towards how ideas are treated to determine whether those ideas are valid," Paladin said. "In school, if students are told the ski club can meet, the French club can meet and the band club can meet but that the Christian club cannot meet, that very fact sends a message that Christianity is not to be tolerated. It sends a message that Christianity is dangerous, out of bounds and is not a valid argument. The EAA is necessary to allow Christianity to be heard in the marketplace of ideas."

Gay and Lesbian Student Clubs

The raging debate over gay and lesbian student clubs often features Equal Access Act disputes. In some communities, students have formed gay and lesbian or gay-straight alliance clubs to promote greater tolerance toward gays and lesbians. These clubs have often met harsh resistance from other students, parents, community leaders and school officials.

In another 2003 case, *Boyd County High School Gay-Straight Alliance v. Board of Education of Boyd County*, a federal judge in Kentucky ruled that school officials violated the Equal Access Act when they refused to give a gay-straight alliance club the same opportunities as other noncurriculum-related student clubs. The stated purpose of the

Jeff Vessels (far right), executive director of the American Civil Liberties Union of Kentucky, is backed by the six students who brought suit against the Boyd County Board of Education because their rights had been violated under the federal Equal Access Act.

club was "to provide students with a safe haven to talk about anti-gay harassment and to work together to promote tolerance, understanding and acceptance of one another regardless of sexual orientation."

The school argued that it was justified in preventing the club from meeting because of the disruptions caused by other students who vigorously opposed the club. These students protested by wearing shirts saying "Adam and Eve, not Adam and Steve." On one school day, half of the students did not attend, many in protest of the gay-straight club. These disruptions caused school officials to suspend all noncurriculum-related [clubs].

However, the gay-straight alliance alleged that school officials, despite the school board's supposed suspension of clubs, still allowed many student groups to meet at Boyd County High School. These clubs included the Drama Club, the Bible Club, the Executive Councils and the Beta Club.

The Issue of Disruption

U.S. District Judge David L. Bunning sided with the student club, finding that school officials violated the Equal Access Act by treating the gay-straight alliance group differently from other student clubs. The judge rejected the school board's argument that it could prohibit the gay-straight club because it caused substantial disruption of school activities under the Equal Access Act.

The judge also said that the Equal Access Act and the famous black-armband case *Tinker v. Des Moines Independent Community School District* from 1969 both allow school officials to prohibit student expression or activities that cause a substantial disruption of school activities. (The Equal Access Act is modeled on the language of the *Tinker* opinion.) However, Bunning reasoned that the *Tinker* case does not allow school officials to suppress student speech based on a heckler's veto. In other words, school officials cannot allow the protesting students to shut down the gay-straight alliance club. The judge wrote that the Equal Access Act would permit school officials to treat the club differently from other clubs "only upon a showing that Plaintiffs' (the gay-straight club) own disruptive activities have interfered with Defendants' (school officials') ability to maintain order and discipline."

Bunning added that "there was no evidence presented during the hearing that either GSA (the gay-straight club) members or GSA Club meetings were disruptive."

The *Boyd* case was settled in 2004. The school agreed to treat the gay-straight club the same as other student clubs, and it agreed to provide training about various types of harassment, including anti-gay harassment.

The Importance of the Equal Access Act

Paul Cates, public education director for the Lesbian and Gay Rights Project of the American Civil Liberties Union, says the Equal Access Act is vital for gay students. "The act has proven critical in erecting safe places where gay and straight students alike can meet and discuss issues like anti-gay harassment and other ways of protecting gay students who often face hostile environments in their high schools."

The Equal Access Act serves a vital purpose in public schools by allowing many student groups to meet even though some may disagree with their ideologies, religions or politics. It enables interested students to assemble to discuss ideas, projects and goals.

In essence, the Equal Access Act furthers education and may even promote greater tolerance in schools. Continuing disputes over Bible clubs and gay-lesbian clubs show the continued need for this important federal law. School officials also run the risk of violating the First Amendment in general if they discriminate against a particular club on the basis of its viewpoint.

EVALUATING THE AUTHOR'S ARGUMENTS:

In this viewpoint David L. Hudson Jr. discusses how the judge in *Boyd County High School Gay-Straight Alliance v. Board of Education of Boyd County* rejected the argument that disruption caused by protestors of a student club is enough for the school to shut it down. What is the difference between disruption caused by a student club itself and disruption caused by protestors of a student club? Do you agree that the difference is important? Why or why not?

Schools Should Not Allow Gay-Straight Alliance Clubs

"Explicit bans or policies banning sexuality clubs or requiring parental consent are effective and can withstand legal challenges if adopted appropriately."

Stephanie Evans

In the following viewpoint Stephanie Evans argues that student gay-straight alliance clubs should be banned in schools. Evans claims that such clubs are political tools used to advance a pro-homosexual platform, and that such clubs are harmful to students. Evans urges parents and educators to oppose gay-straight alliance clubs through pursuit of two exceptions to the Equal Access Act. Evans was a legal intern for the North Carolina Family Policy Council during the summer of 2006, when this article was written.

AS YOU READ, CONSIDER THE FOLLOWING QUESTIONS:

1. According to Evans, what year did gay-straight alliance (GSA) clubs appear in public schools?
2. Evans argues that a primary goal of GSAs is to assure teens what?
3. According to the author, what two exceptions were added to the Equal Access Act (EAA) to allow educator discretion about student clubs?

During the 2005-2006 school year a small group of students at South Rowan High School in China Grove, North Carolina, petitioned their principal for permission to start a gay-straight alliance (GSA). The request immediately sparked controversy and culminated in over 700 concerned parents, students, and community leaders gathering to protest the formation of the GSA.[1] The public outcry convinced the School Board to adopt a policy banning all sexuality clubs, "based upon any sexual grouping or activity of any kind."[2] Organizers of the GSA have threatened to challenge the decision in court, claiming that the policy violates the federal Equal Access Act (EAA). The School Board has not yielded to the threats and is prepared to defend the policy in the event of a lawsuit.[3] If in fact challenged, the legal battle over South Rowan's sexuality policy could have important implications for North Carolina public schools.

Today, in America's public high schools, and even middle schools, after school clubs are no longer limited to the debate team and chorus—students now have access to a variety of activities, including homosexual fellowship and activism. As the homosexual movement continues to meet political and social resistance, activists are increasingly adopting strategies designed to instill tolerance and acceptance of "alternative" lifestyles in America's most impressionable—its children. Gay-Straight Alliance (GSA) clubs have been a key weapon in the arsenal of the homosexual movement for spreading its message to youth. As GSAs have risen in prominence, concerned parents and school boards in several states have begun to fight their presence in American school systems.

What Is a GSA?

Defined as "in-school, extracurricular groups that support [lesbian, gay, bisexual and transgender] students, and those questioning their sexual orientation or gender identity, and their straight friends and allies," gay-straight alliances first emerged in public schools in 1989.[4] Created by Winston-Salem native Kevin Jennings, now executive director of the Gay, Lesbian, and Straight Education Network (GLSEN), GSAs have become the most "visible and widely adopted" component of GLSEN's "safe schools" initiative.[5] With the help and support of national and state organizations such as GLSEN,

Parents, Family and Friends of Lesbians and Gays (PFLAG) and the Gay-Straight Alliance Network (GSAN), the movement has rapidly grown; currently there are over 3,000 GSAs in schools across the country, including over 50 in North Carolina.[6] While GLSEN and other groups claim that the primary function of GSAs is to create safe, homophobic free school environments and to offer support to homosexual, transgender, and "questioning" students, a study of the goals and training materials of these organizations reveals the other objectives behind the well-coordinated GSA movement.

Students wishing to establish new "student" GSAs in their schools have a plethora of start-up resources to choose from, accessed easily and at no cost from several national and local organizations. GLSEN

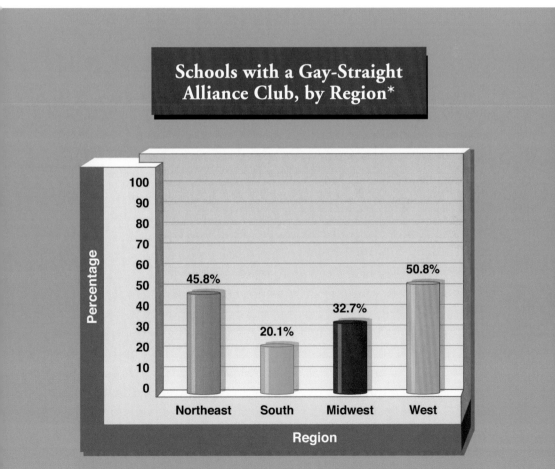

Schools with a Gay-Straight Alliance Club, by Region*

*From a survey of LGBT (lesbian, gay, bisexual, transgender) teenage students in the United States, 2007.

Taken from: J.G. Kosciw, E.M. Diaz, and E.A. Greytak, "2007 National School Climate Survey: The Experiences of Lesbian, Gay, Bisexual, and Transgender Youth in Our Nation's Schools," Gay, Lesbian, and Straight Education Network (GLSEN), 2008.

offers a "Jump-Start" Guide for getting clubs off the ground, complete with recruitment strategies and games to play at initial interest meetings. The guide, along with other materials, can be sent to any student upon request.[7] GSAN's website provides students with 25 "How To" manuals offering advice about creating a "Kick A** GSA."[8] In North Carolina, several organizations aid and develop student GSAs. Safe Schools N.C. holds leadership summits for interested teens, and the Triangle Gay Straight Alliance Network will send trainers to local high schools to spark student interest or boost fledgling GSAs.[9]

Once formed, GSAs are encouraged not only to improve the school's "homosexual climate," but to push for gay-friendly curricula, participate in political activism campaigns, and develop relationships with local adult homosexual groups.[10] GLSEN promotes "Teach the Teacher" workshops where GSA members train faculty on "queering the curriculum"—which is inserting homosexual issues into academic subjects such as English and math and implementing the use of "gender-friendly" language in the classroom.[11]

Student GSAs are also urged to become politically active. GSAN provides a strategy chart for organizing GSA campaigns, outlining ways to "mobilize your constituents and allies" and "put pressure on targets to respond."[12] GSAs across the country are recruited to hold homosexual events and "awareness days." GLSEN touts that their annual "Day of Silence" campaign, where students are called to stand against homosexual harassment, is one of the largest "student-led" actions in American history, with over 4,000 participating schools.[13]

Alarmingly, community gay and lesbian organizations are also sold to GSAs as places where they can find "supportive" homosexual adults willing to mentor and offer friendship. GSAN manuals suggest students attend local lesbian, gay, bisexual, transgender, and questioning (LGBTQ) dances for club outings.[14] GLSEN advises new GSAs to chapters and invite adult members of local GLSEN and PFLAG organizations to meetings as guest speakers.[15] In North Carolina, the Triangle Chapter of PFLAG is closely involved with area high schools—it frequently holds student panels and actively fundraises for GSAs in the Raleigh area.[16]

As materials offered by groups like GLSEN reveal, GSAs are not merely school social clubs that gather for meetings once or twice a month to offer support and encouragement to members. Rather,

GSAs are tools of national organizations that train students to be well-oiled machines, prepped to advance the homosexual political and social agenda. In promoting GSAs, national homosexual advocacy groups have found a breeding ground for a new generation of activists—America's public schools.

The Harms of GSAs

Targeting adolescents when confusion about sexuality is at its peak, GSAs promote sex and homosexuality to youth while ignoring and denying the physical and emotional risks of the homosexual lifestyle. Furthermore, GSAs encourage relationships between youth and adult homosexuals and that undermine the moral and religious teachings of parents.

A primary goal of GSAs is to assure teens that homosexuality is normal and acceptable. This "it's ok to be gay" mentality teaches that those opposed to homosexual behaviors are either old fashioned or bigoted. At many schools, GSA members who are confused about their sexuality are offered counseling through outside organizations such as Triangle PFLAG, which teach that homosexuality is natural and simply a matter of genetics.[17]

Typically, GSAs are also supportive of sexual exploration. Many GSAs offer information through gay websites where they can learn about sex. Glenn High School's GSA, in Kernersville, N.C., has several links on its website leading students to information on anal sex, emergency contraceptives and abortion. Across the Glenn High GSA site advertisements for homosexual personals run. Recently "Local Sex Photo Personals" on Xmatch.com. were promoted.[18]

Conveniently, warnings about the risks and dangers of homosexual behavior are noticeably lacking from the message GSAs extend to students. Instead, the homosexual lifestyle is celebrated while the evidence documenting its destructive consequences is ignored or denied.

Those who engage in homosexual acts are at higher risks for sexually transmitted diseases (STDs), including HIV and AIDS, anal cancer, substance abuse, suicide, and depression.[19] Instead of being warned that homosexuality is harmful to their physical and emotional health, students in GSAs are often told that ignorance and intolerance are to blame for the increased STD, depression and suicide rates in homosexuals. Groups like GLSEN claim that GSAs are needed to teach teens about "safe" sex, and to provide social outlets and support networks to combat the depression associated with adolescent homosexuality. However, numerous studies have shown that programs promoting safe sex have done nothing to decrease STD infection among teens and international research indicates that the promotion of homosexuality fails to help depression or suicide problems in homosexuals.[20] Findings show that in countries where homosexuality is widely accepted, increased depression and suicide rates among homosexuals are equal if not greater to U.S. rates.[21]

In addition to the skewed messages about homosexuality GSAs present, the relationships encouraged between GSAs and adult homosexual community organizations can severely harm students. Once GSAs become involved with local gay organizations, they have access to conferences, seminars, social events, and even dating services that gay community centers offer. These events are beyond a school's jurisdiction, so subject matters and materials covered have no content restrictions or standards. Furthermore, most gay community centers do not require students to have parental permission to participate in events, they only need to show that they are "under 22."[22] In fact, some organizations even discourage youth from telling their parents about their involvement with the group, or their sexuality. A brochure entitled "Be Yourself" from PFLAG portrays parents as homophobic and possibly dangerous. It warns students that they should not "come out" until they have a safe place to go because parents may become abusive or force them to leave home after learning about their homosexual behavior.[23]

The following is a mere sampling of some of the activities student members of GSAs have had access to through local gay community organizations:

- A "Make Your Own Sex Toy Night."[24]
- "Queer Colleges." A course entitled "HIV" was listed with this description: *SEX! Yeah, we know you're doing it. . . . We'll have open, honest, judgment-free conversations about sex toys, oral sex, bare-backing, mixing sex and drugs, how to keep it safe and advocate for yourself during group sex, anonymous sex, and sex on the go!*[25]
- Time Out Youth, a gay youth organization in the Charlotte-Metro area holds overnight "lock-ins" for teens with "gender

variant identities." On its website, detailed descriptions on how to use condoms are given. In May 2006 the group hosted workshops on homosexual activism, safe sex and HIV testing.[26]

Protecting Students from GSAs

Realizing the harmful effects these clubs have on teens, parents across the country have voiced concern and school boards and policymakers have taken action to stop the groups, but until recently their success has been limited.

Since the GSA movement began, groups like Lambda Legal and the American Civil Liberties Union (ACLU) have become skilled at evoking the federal Equal Access Act (EAA) to defend the rights of GSAs in public schools. The EAA, passed in 1984, states that schools cannot discriminate against non-curricular student groups "on basis of religious, political, philosophical, or other speech context."[27] The Act, which has been used by several Christian organizations to fight religious discrimination, calls for school systems to treat all non-curricular

The Equal Access Act was originally designed to protect the rights of extracurricular groups in schools, which can include gay-straight alliance clubs. However, some people oppose support of gay rights.

school groups equally, or not recognize any at all. Where GSA bans have been challenged, the EAA has often been used to force school boards to permit GSAs. However, as GSAs have become more prevalent, and parents and educators more aware of the threats they pose, some strategies have been effective in keeping GSAs out of public schools.

Banning "Sexuality" Clubs. Unlike clubs related to academics or sports, the identities of GSAs are premised upon one unifying characteristic: sexuality. Federal courts have ruled that even though "the EAA prohibits discrimination on the basis of content . . . if schools treated all clubs the same with respect to the issue in question, the regulation of content might be permissible."[28] This interpretation has encouraged school administrators to adopt "no sexuality-based clubs" policies, where all students are prohibited from forming organizations that relate to any sexual topic—heterosexuality, homosexuality, polygamy, bestiality, prostitution, pornography, etc.

While successful in shutting out GSAs from school campuses, this approach is not ideal because it prevents the formation of clubs that support and promote healthy and responsible sexual decision-making. In the last decade, abstinence clubs, which encourage students to postpone sexual relationships until marriage, have been surfacing in schools. Several Christian student clubs also have members take abstinence pledges. A ban against sexuality clubs could silence the healthy message these groups extend to teens.

Parental Consent Laws. Another tactic in the fight against GSAs is enacting parental consent regulations. These provisions give parents the ability to prevent their children from becoming involved with dangerous or harmful organizations like GSAs. In most proposed parental consent policies, parents must sign written consent forms granting their children permission to participate in after school groups. Not surprisingly, GSA advocates lobby hard to have the laws blocked when they are raised in state legislatures or promoted as policy by local school boards. Activists claim that requiring written parental permission would discourage homosexual students with "oppressive" or "intolerant" parents from seeking support in GSAs. These arguments reveal the true feelings of GSA proponents—that parents do not know what is best for their children and that GSAs and other homosexual organizations are better able to offer youth support and instruction.

However, like bans on sexuality clubs, parental consent laws have their drawbacks. GSAs can still be formed in schools with these policies, which means that the opportunity for their harmful messages and activities to reach students still exists. Even if the consent requirements severely hamper GSA membership, it only takes a few students to establish a club, solicit help from organizations like GLSEN and begin lobbying school administrations for curriculum changes and activities that affect the entire school.

GSA Bans and EAA Exceptions. The best option in protecting students from the harms of GSAs are explicit bans of the organizations. Although some federal courts, like those in Utah and Kentucky, have ruled that GSAs fall under the blanket of protection of the EAA, two EAA exceptions have become important in defending bans against GSAs.

When the EAA was proposed in Congress, legislators were concerned that the Act could be used to establish student organizations like GSAs and would limit the ability of educators to apply appropriate discretion when recognizing after school groups that may endanger students or the educational process. To remedy these problems, two exceptions to the EAA were added. The Maintaining Order and Discipline and Well-being-of-the-Students exceptions state that "nothing [in the EAA] should be construed to limit the authority of the school, its agents or employees, to maintain order and discipline on school premises, to protect the well-being of students and faculty, and to assure that attendance at meetings is voluntary."[29]

Under these exceptions strong arguments can be made against allowing students to form GSAs. In states like North Carolina, with laws against sodomy and indecent liberties with minors, the Maintaining Order and Discipline exception is applicable because GSAs condone and even promote the acts criminalized in state statutes. Clearly, it would be extremely hard for schools to maintain order if clubs promoting the contravention of state law were allowed to meet on campus. Just as school administrators would be justified in denying recognition to a student marijuana club because it would encourage students to break the law, schools in states with sodomy statutes should be entitled to ban GSAs because of their connection to unlawful activity.

In addition, the U.S. Supreme Court has said that through the Maintaining Order and Discipline exception, "the [EAA] does not limit a school's authority to expressly prohibit meetings that would 'materially and substantially interfere with the orderly conduct of educational activities within the school.'"[30] GSA meetings certainly have the potential to interfere with educational activities. The messages sent by GSAs stand in stark opposition with N.C. law requiring abstinence-until-marriage education in public schools. Advice students receive through their involvement with GSAs concerning sex methods, "safer sex" options, and contraception directly opposes an abstinence curriculum and disrupts the educational process by sending conflicting messages to students. The tension and controversy GSAs often create in schools also distracts students from learning as attention is diverted from academics to the political and social turmoil over the GSA in the school and community.

The Well-being-of-the-Students exception of the EAA also provides a solid basis for denying GSAs a place in public schools. The EAA was not created to interfere with what the Supreme Court has recognized as an important duty of the public school system—providing for the well being of children.[31]

As a guardian of children's well-being, schools have an interest in protecting students from the physical, mental, and emotional harms of increased sexual activity. Through their promotion of homosexuality and so-called "safe sex," GSAs expose students to lifestyles that put them at higher risk for HIV and other STDs, anal cancer, depression and suicide. Prohibiting GSAs protects children from the dangerous—and possibly deadly—messages they convey to adolescents. Therefore, banning organizations that promote risky behaviors and expose students to obscene sexual material is responsible policymaking.

In light of these exceptions, bans on GSAs make sense, especially in states where sodomy or indecent liberties with minors laws or in schools where abstinence-only education policies are in place.

However, advocates of GSAs, like the ACLU, are quick to challenge bans in court, on the basis that the they violate the EAA. Until recently, lawyers defending GSAs have been successful in convincing courts to interpret the EAA in a way that labels bans of GSAs unlawful, but the legal tide may be turning. Recently, a federal court ruled that the Lubbock Independent School District was within its rights under the EAA when it adopted a policy prohibiting sexuality clubs. The ban was instituted after students at Lubbock High applied to form a GSA. The School District based its argument defending the ban on two premises. First, that the Maintaining Order and Discipline exception to the EAA was applicable due to the District's abstinence-only education policy and Texas Penal Codes outlawing certain forms of homosexual activity and sexual relations among minors. Second, the District maintained that under the Well-being-of-the-Students provision of the EAA, they were entitled to ban sexuality-based groups like the Lubbock High GSA because their promotion of homosexuality and "safe sex" put public school students at mental, physical, and emotional risk. The court agreed with the District, stating,

> [T]his case has nothing to do with a denial of rights to students because of their sexual viewpoints. It is instead an assertion of a school's right not to surrender control of the public school system to students and erode a community's standard of what subject matter is considered obscene and inappropriate. At some point, a line must be drawn that considers the proper subject matter allowed in the schools of this country. The effects of exposing minors to sexual material before they are mature enough to understand its consequences and far-reaching psychological ramifications compels a school district to step in and draw such a line. This case is simply about a school district's ability to control sexual subject matter on its campus.[32]

The court noted that the District's abstinence-only education policy was essential to the legality of the ban, and that excluding GSAs may not be appropriate under the EAA in school systems without an abstinence policy. The fact that Texas had strong laws in place against the activities promoted by GSAs also heavily influenced the court's decision.

Like the Lubbock School District, North Carolina also has a state-wide abstinence-until-marriage education policy.[33] In order for school administrators to have a firm basis for banning GSAs, the maintenance of this policy is crucial because it clearly sets a standard that keeps the promotion of sex before marriage out of the school. North Carolina's laws against sodomy and crimes against nature, as well as statutes criminalizing indecent liberties with minors, also give strong support to policymakers wishing to implement regulations prohibiting GSAs. Without these statutes the argument that GSAs promote and encourage minors to participate in illegal behavior is lost.

Conclusion

As the homosexual movement has found, students are a captive audience, easily able to absorb the messages of the homosexual agenda. GSAs are a key component of this socialization process, but parents, educators and legislators are not powerless against their assaults on North Carolina students.

To stop the influence of GSAs, parents must be informed and vocal, ready to approach school officials about developing policies prohibiting the clubs. Educators must also be willing to take a stand against the coordinated efforts of the GSA movement. Contrary to the claims of the ACLU, the EAA does not absolutely guarantee the rights of GSAs in public schools. Explicit bans or policies banning sexuality clubs or requiring parental consent are effective and can withstand legal challenges if adopted appropriately. Local education policies, and better yet, statewide legislation banning GSAs, would give all North Carolina students protection against the threats they pose.

While claiming to be harmless clubs that offer support to struggling youth and fight harassment, GSAs promote a message of sex and homosexuality that puts public school students at mental, emotional, and physical risk while undermining parental moral and religious teachings. North Carolinians need to be aware of the dangers of GSAs and prepared to develop policies and laws that prevent GSAs from endangering children.

EVALUATING THE AUTHORS' ARGUMENTS:

In this viewpoint Stephanie Evans urges pursuit of banning student gay-straight alliance clubs, or GSAs, through two exceptions to the Equal Access Act. How might David L. Hudson Jr., author of the previous viewpoint, argue that GSAs should not be prohibited in this way?

Endnotes

1. Christian Newswire, "Radical Homosexual Agenda Reeling in Charlotte," Michnews.com, April 12, 2006, www.michnews.com/cgi-bin/artman/exec/view.cgi/278/12457.
2. Extracurricular Activities Policy. Adopted by the Rowan-Salisbury Board of Education. August 14, 2006.
3. Valle, Kirsten. "South students can challenge gay club ban, group says." *Salisbury Post.* April 12, 2006.
4. Cianciotto, Jason and Sean Cahill. *Education Policy: Issues Affecting Lesbian, Gay, Bisexual, and Transgender Youth.* National Gay and Lesbian Task Force Policy Institute. 2003. pg.114.
5. ElHage, Alysse, "Homosexual Indoctrination: How Safety is Used to Promote Homosexuality in Schools." *Findings.* North Carolina Family Policy Council. December, 2004.
6. "Welcome to the Student's Resource Page," Gay, Lesbian, and Straight Education Network (GLSEN). www.glsen.org.
7. Ibid. "Students."
8. "GSA Resources." Gay-Straight Alliance Network (GSAN). www.gsanetwork.org.
9. "Invite TGSAN to Your School," Triangle Gay-Straight Alliance Network. www.safeschoolsnc.com/tgsannew/details.asp?ID=6.
10. "Overview of Gay-Straight Alliances." GLSEN. www.glsen.org.
11. "20 Ways Your GSA Can Rock the World." GSAN. www.gsanetwork.org.
12. "Developing a Strategy." GSAN. www.gsanetwork.org.

13. "Thousands of Schools Participate in GLSEN's 10th Annual Day of Silence." GLSEN. April 26, 2006.
14. "Fun Things To Do With Your GSA," GSAN. www.gsanetwork.org.
15. *Gay-Straight Alliance Handbook.* GLSEN. pg. 3. Available online at www.glsen.org.
16. "Advocacy." Triangle Parents and Friends of Lesbians and Gays North Carolina. http://www.pflagtriangle.org/advocacy.html.
17. Ibid. "Education."
18. Glenn High School GSA "Resources" Page, gsaglenn.tripod.com /id13.html. Viewed on 7/10/06.
19. ElHage, Alysse, "The Health Risks of Sodomy," *Findings.* North Carolina Family Policy Council, January 2000.
20. ElHage, Alysse, "The Case for Abstinence," *Findings.* North Carolina Family Policy Council, April 2002.
21. Whitehead, N.E., Ph D., "Homosexuality and Mental Health Problems," April 2006, www.narth.com/docs/whitehead.html.
22. Harvey, Linda, "How Homosexual School Clubs Offer Sex to Students," www.worldnetdaily.com.
23. ElHage, Alysse. "Homosexual Indoctrination: How Safety is Used to Promote Homosexuality in Schools," *Findings.* North Carolina Family Policy Council, December 2004, pg. 2.
24. Ibid.
25. BAGLY, *QuAC Institute for Social Justice Course Catalog.* www.bagly.org/quac/, pg. 4.
26. Time Out Youth, www.timeoutyouth.org,
27. The Equal Access Act, 20 U.S.C. § 4071(a).
28. *Franklin Cent. Gay/Straight Alliance v. Franklin Twp. Cmty. Sch. Corp.,* 2002 U.S. Dist. LEXIS 24981 (S.D. Ind. 2002)(emphasis added).
29. Op cit. EAA, § 4071(f).
30. *Westside Cmty. Bd. Of Educ. v. Mergens,* 496 U.S. 226, quoting the EAA, 20 U.S.C. § 4071(c)(4).
31. *Bellotti v. Baird,* 443 U.S. 622 (1979)(inner quotes and citations omitted).
32. *Caudillo v. Lubbock Independent Sch. Dist.,* 311 F. Supp. 2d 550 (N. D. TX 2004).
33. N.C. Gen. Stat. § 115C-81(4)(a)(2006).

Chapter 2

Are School Safety Policies Warranted?

High school students at a rally in New York demand a role in school safety policies.

Federal and State Law Require Zero Tolerance School Policies

"In California, governing boards have found that it is important for each school district to align zero tolerance sanctions with state and federal law."

California Department of Education

In the following viewpoint the California Department of Education contends that both federal law and state law require zero tolerance policies. The author argues that the justification for zero tolerance policies was to cut down on school shootings. The California Department of Education claims that it is not this goal but, rather, certain methods used to implement the policy that have created controversy about zero tolerance policies. The author suggests guidelines for avoiding misplaced application of zero tolerance policies. The California Department of Education is the California agency that oversees public education.

Although the term zero tolerance does not appear in law, the Federal Gun-Free Schools Act of 1994 requires school districts across the United States to pass what came to be labeled zero tolerance policies for firearms in order to remain eligible for funds. The Act requires one calendar year of expulsion for any student bringing a firearm to school and referral of the student to law enforcement.

The California Legislature amended *Education Code (EC)* Section 48915 (c) to fulfill the federal mandate. California law also adds a requirement for the mandatory suspension and the recommendation for expulsion of students who:

- Possess, sell, or otherwise furnish a firearm
- Brandish a knife at another person
- Sell a controlled substance
- Commit or attempt to commit a sexual assault or sexual battery
- Possess an explosive

EC Section 48906 includes the requirement to refer a student with a firearm to law enforcement, and California *EC* Section 48915 requires the school district governing board to refer students who commit the above acts to an alternative program of study that meets the standards listed within the section.

The Rationale for Establishing Zero Tolerance Policies

Given public concern about escalating incidences of school violence, and in the wake of school shootings, school district governing boards

School district governing boards have adopted zero tolerance safety policies in response to school shootings.

adopted zero tolerance policies to send a "get tough" message to the community that violent behavior, incidents, and crime would not be tolerated. Policies were adopted that advised there would be no tolerating more common causes of expulsion, which are listed in *EC* Section 48915(a). For these offenses, the law states that the principal or superintendent may find that "expulsion is inappropriate due to the particular circumstance." These significant but discretionary infractions include:

- Causing serious physical injury to another person, except in self-defense
- Possession of any knife or other dangerous object of no reasonable use to the pupil
- Unlawful possession of any controlled substance, except for the possession of not more than one ounce of marijuana
- Robbery or extortion
- Assault or battery on any school employee

These infractions require that the decision to expel a student be based on one of the following findings:

1. Other means of correction are not feasible or have repeatedly failed to bring about proper conduct.
2. Due to the nature of the act, the presence of the pupil causes continuing danger to the physical safety of the pupil or others. . . .

The Methods and Goals of Zero Tolerance

Since its inception, zero tolerance has received mixed reactions. Most of the controversy has been created by the *methods* being used to implement this policy rather than the *goals* that school districts hoped to achieve by adopting zero tolerance policies.

What appeared to be a catch-all solution has educators going in a lot of different directions. Relatively trivial incidents in a school setting (minor fights, possession of organic cough drops) that receive media attention have given the overall impression that local practice extends zero tolerance beyond its original intent, and school officials are being warned that zero tolerance policies will not stop tragic school shootings like those that occurred in Columbine, Colorado and elsewhere. Additionally, a policy that does not allow school administrators' discretion or consideration may be ruled by the courts as arbitrary and capricious and found to be in violation of a student's due process rights.

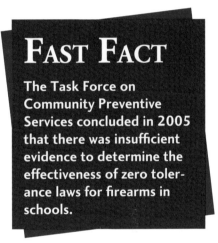

FAST FACT

The Task Force on Community Preventive Services concluded in 2005 that there was insufficient evidence to determine the effectiveness of zero tolerance laws for firearms in schools.

A zero tolerance study conducted by the Civil Rights Project at Harvard University states that, in addition to the risk of students being unfairly punished, a disproportionate number of minority students are being affected by zero tolerance policies. For example, the report states that data collected from South Carolina shows black students accounted for 61 percent of disciplinary code violations, even though they make up only 42 percent of public school enrollment.

"School shooting," cartoon by Ed Fischer, www.CartoonStock.com. Copyright © Ed Fischer. Reproduction rights available from www.CartoonStock.com.

Zero Tolerance Discipline Policies

In California, governing boards have found that it is important for each school district to align zero tolerance sanctions with state and federal law. Further, the most difficult part of an expulsion hearing is not determining whether the act was committed but whether *findings* can be made concerning other means of correction or the potential danger to the student or others.

The Civil Rights Project report offers the following recommendations for administering zero tolerance discipline policies:

- Monitor disciplinary referrals and keep careful records to ensure that teachers do not overreact or unfairly single out students. Teachers who engage in such practices should be required to take professional development courses in classroom management, child development, and multicultural human relations.
- Require training in classroom management and behavioral issues, including familiarity with legal requirements and their fairness.
- Establish a minimum number of staff development days devoted to classroom management, guidance techniques, and conflict

resolution; the classroom management plan should relate to the seriousness of school discipline issues and should be reviewed periodically.

- Develop in-school suspension programs to keep students on track with schoolwork and provide counseling, including sessions about behavior modification and conflict resolution. Recent reductions in counseling and social work budgets in many districts should be reversed.

EVALUATING THE AUTHOR'S ARGUMENTS:

In this viewpoint the California Department of Education identifies six scenarios, one required by federal law and five by California state law, that allow for zero tolerance. Do you think that zero tolerance is justified in these scenarios? Why or why not?

Viewpoint
2

Zero Tolerance Policies Are Not Effective

Paul G. Mattiuzzi

"In the school, I believe that a zero-tolerance policy sends exactly the wrong message."

In the following viewpoint Paul G. Mattiuzzi contends that zero tolerance policies are not appropriate tools of discipline in school. Mattiuzzi reviews recent research, arguing that this research shows that five assumptions about zero tolerance policies are mistaken. Moreover, he argues that research shows the policies are not only ineffective but actually harmful. Mattiuzzi concludes that discipline needs to be handed out with discretion and that zero tolerance policies do not allow for this. Mattiuzzi is a psychologist who authors the blog *EverydayPsychology.com*, which comments on recent psychological research.

AS YOU READ, CONSIDER THE FOLLOWING QUESTIONS:
1. The author contends that despite an assumption to the contrary, school violence rates have done what over the last twenty years?
2. According to Mattiuzzi, does the research about zero tolerance policies support or dispute the claim that they are colorblind?
3. The author contends that one danger of zero tolerance policies is that offenders do what rather than take responsibility for their behavior?

The term "zero tolerance" suggests that it is a consistent, no-nonsense approach, and that such policies must therefore obviously be an effective and beneficial disciplinary strategy. These policies are prominent in the educational system, and so in the interest of school accountability, it is relevant to ask: Does it really work?

The American Psychological Association [APA] considered that question and created a task force to look at the data and the research. Recently published [2009] in the *American Psychologist*, the Task Force report suggests that when put to the test, the policy flunks.

Flawed Assumptions About Zero Tolerance

The analysis focused on five key assumptions underlying the use of zero tolerance policies in the schools:

1. It is assumed that zero tolerance policies are necessary because school violence is increasing and increasingly out of control. The reality is that the rates of violence and disruption in schools have remained steady or have actually declined over the past twenty years or so. Obviously, violence prevention efforts are absolutely necessary to protect against both commonplace incidents and critical acts of aggression. However, disciplinary policies should be formulated in response to the actual threat, and not in response to the "feeling" that the problem is out of control.

2. It is also assumed that mandatory and inflexible punishments serve to create consistent discipline and clarity in the disciplinary message. In fact, they do not. *Within school districts* that have adopted such policies, there remains a great deal of variation across schools with respect to how many kids are actually disciplined (or need to be disciplined), and there is just as much variation *across school districts* with similar policies. Whether or not a school is orderly has much less to do with the disciplinary guidelines than with the quality of teachers and the quality of school governance. Indeed, the quality of the school may be more important than the attitudes and behavior of the students.

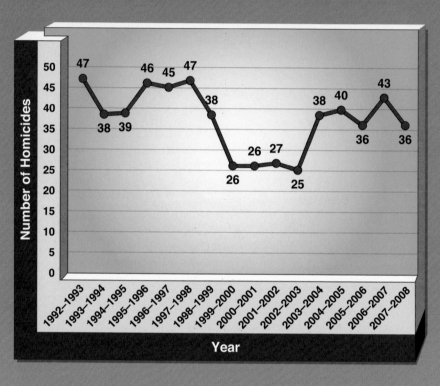

Number of US School-Associated Homicides of Students, Staff, and Nonstudents, 1992–2008

Taken from: IES National Center for Education Statistics, "Indicators of School Crime and Safety: 2009."/Centers for Disease Control and Prevention, 1992–2008 School-Associated Violent Deaths Surveillance Study, partially funded by the US Department of Education, Office of Safe and Drug-Free Schools, previously unpublished tabulation (July 2009).

3. It is assumed that the removal of disruptive students provides for a school climate more conducive to learning. In fact, the opposite is true. Schools in which expulsions and suspensions are common tend to have *less* satisfactory school climate ratings and are found to spend a disproportionate amount of time on disciplinary issues. And after taking into account the socio-economic status of students, they tend to have lower academic achievement rates.

4. It is assumed that zero tolerance punishments will deter those expelled or suspended from misbehaving in the future. Instead, what is found is that those who are disciplined in this fashion will in the future be more likely to continue misbehaving, more

likely to drop-out and less likely to graduate. Perhaps it would be justified if some benefit accrued to the school and the student body, but it is not justified if it simply involves making it a problem to be dealt with by someone else.

5. The final assumption considered is the idea that parents and students overwhelmingly support zero-tolerance policies. Here, the data are mixed. Some parents applaud such efforts, especially when the punishment is applied in specific cases that have caused public alarm. On the other hand, there are just as many cases in which parents and other students are left feeling that the punishment was unfair and that some measure of forbearance should have been granted. The concept of "a second chance" is deeply rooted in our consciousness, as is the idea that "the punishment should fit the crime."

FAST FACT

In late 2009, a six-year-old boy was ordered by a Delaware school district to attend an alternative school for bringing a Cub Scout dinner knife to eat his lunch.

School discipline is important. Punishments are often necessary. If it could be shown that arbitrary rules made schools safer or that they eased the administrative burdens associated with exercising discipline, then of course a zero tolerance approach would be recommended. But what seems to make sense does not always in fact meet the test of common sense.

The Dark Side of Zero Tolerance

After considering whether or not zero tolerance policies have any unique benefit, the APA Task Force also looked at whether there is a downside or dark side to such policies.

On the dark side, there are important implications. First, it appears quite certain that rather than being "color blind," arbitrary punishment strategies tend to disproportionately affect students of color and students who suffer from various forms of psychological disturbance. Second, there is clear evidence that zero tolerance policies tend to increase the likelihood that those disciplined will end up as clients of

The author argues that zero tolerance policies in schools have been shown to be ineffective and possibly harmful. Here Gene Buinger, superintendent of a school district in Texas, answers questions about his district's zero tolerance policy.

either the juvenile justice or criminal justice system. In general, these policies violate the old adage: "An ounce of prevention is worth a pound of cure."

The APA Task Force did not in any way seek to suggest that disciplinary actions are unimportant, or to argue for excuse and tolerance. Instead, they outlined a set of recommendations focused on the benefits of flexibility. In any situation where a disciplinary response is required, there are indeed different and "alternative strategies" to be considered.

With respect to making schools safe, the weight of the evidence shows that there is little benefit to be obtained from abandoning individual case analysis and judgment. There is no apparent benefit to be obtained from arbitrary rules. There are in fact a number of disciplinary alternatives available in any situation. The task is to evaluate every situation on its own merits.

The Need for Judgment and Discretion

Further comment: As a long-time observer of the criminal justice system, I am particularly aware of the fact that arbitrary rules are counter-productive. Set rules do not provide respect for authority. Justice demands that every crime and every offender should be judged individually. That is what Judges should do.

Arbitrary rules serve to diminish the role of Judges. In the school setting, arbitrary rules serve to diminish the role of the School Principal.

From my perspective, the danger presented by zero tolerance policies (and mandatory sentencing guidelines) is that they provide the offender with an excuse and a justification. Rather than taking responsibility for their behavior, they blame the system for its rigidity. There is hardly anything more dangerous than an offender who believes the system did not afford them justice. Rather than having the punishment serve to correct their behavior, the belief that they were treated unfairly is used as a justification for future misbehavior.

And in the school, I believe that a zero-tolerance policy sends exactly the wrong message. It is often the case that when someone is expelled simply as a matter of course and in a reflexive way, other students will rally to their cause, rather than condemning their behavior.

Authority figures have a responsibility to exercise judgment and discretion. When they wash their hands and abandon that responsibility, they lose respect and credibility in the eyes of those they are meant to guide.

EVALUATING THE AUTHORS' ARGUMENTS:

In this viewpoint Paul G. Mattiuzzi argues that zero tolerance ends up being arbitrary and does not allow for enough discretion by authorities. In the previous viewpoint, how does the California Department of Education appear to allow for discretion within its zero-tolerance policies? Would Mattiuzzi be in favor of California's zero tolerance policies as they are described?

Student Searches Are Important for Safety

Korrina Grom

"It is a deterrent for these kids when they know there's a possibility of this drug-sniffing dog (finding something)."

In the following viewpoint Korrina Grom reports on the efforts of the Antioch, Illinois, Village Board and local police department to institute random searches of Antioch Community High School grounds and lockers. The school superintendent opposes the searches on grounds of student privacy but indicates a willingness to cooperate if sufficient evidence of need is provided. According to Grom, representatives of the village press the school board for the searches in the interest of student safety. The local police chief provides evidence of drug use by students and argues that searches using department drug- and gunpowder-sniffing dogs are crucial to making the schools in the district safer. Grom was a staff writer for the *Antioch Review* in Yellow Springs, Ohio.

AS YOU READ, CONSIDER THE FOLLOWING QUESTIONS:
1. What is the difference between Antioch Community High School and Antioch Upper Grade School, according to police Chief Charlie Watkins?
2. Who is Dennis Hockney and what is his position on random searches?
3. Who is Eric Skoog and how does he help or hinder the use of random searches at Antioch Community High School?

A string of drug arrests in and near Antioch Community High School [in Antioch, Illinois] has re-ignited the issue of using drug-sniffing dogs to randomly search student lockers.

Antioch's Village Board is drafting a letter to high school officials asking them to reconsider allowing random searches of the grounds and lockers, which are done at Antioch Upper Grade School on a regular basis. Local police Chief Charlie Watkins also went on record urging the school board to allow the searches.

"Almost every high school in Illinois has random searches of lockers in high schools, except for Antioch," he said. "It is a deterrent for these kids when they know there's a possibility of this drug-sniffing dog (finding something)."

Privacy Issue

But Antioch High School Superintendent Dennis Hockney insisted the district is only opposed to random searches, and would be willing to cooperate given sufficient evidence of the need.

"We've never said 'no' (to drug searches). We've been very clear about that," Hockney said. "We're always concerned when there's anything involving drugs in the school. We've been very proactive."

During meetings with police and village officials, he said, school administrators have indicated drug searches would be allowed if sufficient evidence was provided that there was a problem in the school.

Random searches of the school, Hockney said, would violate students' privacy.

"It's a privacy, search and seizure issue," he said.

Hockney said the school surveys students about drug and alcohol use and makes those findings public.

Antioch Village Trustee Scott Pierce said the village attorney has been directed to draft a letter to the high school board requesting permission to do random drug searches.

"The village itself feels very strongly about keeping drugs out of the high school," he said. "It's time to bring this issue to the forefront."

Pierce said residents are encouraged to let the high school board know whether or not they feel random searches are appropriate.

"It's in the interest of (students') safety," Pierce said.

Recent Arrests

The arrests that brought the issue to the forefront began almost two weeks ago. On Oct. 11 [2002], a high school student was arrested near the high school for possession of marijuana. [Lieutenant] Ron

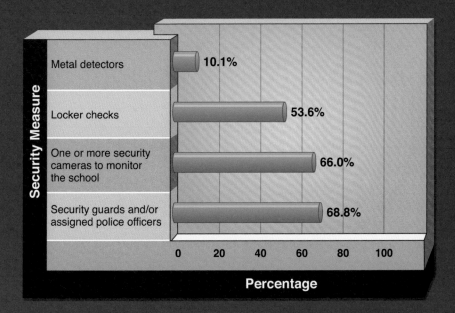

Percentage of Students Aged 12–18 Who Reported Selected Security Measures at School, 2007

Taken from: US Department of Justice, Bureau of Justice Statistics, School Crime Supplement to the National Crime Victimization Survey, various years, 1999–2007.

Police frisk high school students who were found loitering outside their school in Baltimore, Maryland. The Baltimore City public school system works closely with Baltimore police on school security measures.

Roth of the Antioch Police Department said the student admitted to smoking marijuana before school regularly.

Three students were arrested in the high school, one on Oct. 16 and two on Oct. 17, for possession of marijuana, Roth said. One of the students, a female, said she regularly brings drugs to school for personal use, said Roth.

An Antioch Upper Grade School student was taken into custody on Oct. 17 for possession of marijuana and told police she smoked marijuana before arriving at school, Roth said.

The students charged with possession of an illegal substance were referred to juvenile court.

"Drugs at the school we just can't tolerate," said Watkins. "Those who are getting high before school just aren't doing themselves justice."

Many of the arrests were the result of confidential tips or just observing the goings-on at the schools, said Detective Daryl Youngs, who works extensively with Antioch Community High School.

"We do a lot of our work through anonymous information," said Watkins. "Sometimes it's bogus and other times it's dead-on."

The involvement of school administrators in the process, along with searches of the schools by the police department's drug-sniffing dog, are crucial to keeping drugs out of schools, he said.

"(Antioch Upper Grade School Principal Eric Skoog) calls the police department once a week to see how he can make the school safer," said Watkins.

"We couldn't ask for better teamwork," said Youngs.

The police department's K-9 unit did a random sweep of the Antioch Upper Grade School grounds, including 600 lockers, on Oct. 10.

The dog has also been trained to detect gun powder, he said.

EVALUATING THE AUTHORS' ARGUMENTS:

In this viewpoint Korrina Grom presents a case study of a community attempting to institute random searches in one of its high schools. Compare this viewpoint with the following one by Sandy English, who opposes student searches. What is the strength of each viewpoint's argument? How do these differ?

Student Searches Violate the Rights of Students

Sandy English

> *"Students have reacted with indignation at the city's intrusions into their right to privacy."*

In the following viewpoint Sandy English argues that the plan by New York City to subject students to random searches by metal detector is part of a larger trend in the erosion of student rights through school policies. English claims that many students have protested school search policies. She contends that the schools targeted for strict search policies and for increased police presence are schools that serve less affluent students, adding an element of social polarization. English writes for the World Socialist website, published by the International Committee of the Fourth International, the leadership of the world Socialist movement.

Sandy English, "New York City: Random Searches for Public School Students," wsws.org, April 19, 2006. Copyright © 2006 by World Socialist Website. Reproduced by permission.

AS YOU READ, CONSIDER THE FOLLOWING QUESTIONS:
  1. According to English, how many of New York City's public schools have permanent metal detectors?
  2. At a protest at DeWitt Clinton High School in 2005, how many students walked out, according to the author?
  3. English says that the total number of school officers in the New York City school system as of the writing of this piece was how many?

I n a further erosion of democratic rights in New York City, Mayor Michael Bloomberg announced that after April 24, [2006,] School Safety Agents and police officers will perform random searches with metal detectors of students attending the city's middle and high schools. Police Commissioner Raymond Kelly said the searches might affect as many as 10 schools a day, noting that the Police Department already had the necessary material and personnel. The president of the United Federation of Teachers, Randi Weingarten, praised the policy as a "very important first step" and called for the "enforcing of codes of conduct."

Searches with Metal Detectors

Despite the fact that major crime has declined in city schools over the past year, neither students nor school staff will have warning before being scanned, though the city will honor legal obligations by posting the new policy on school buildings. The authorities will not only confiscate guns and knives but also other prohibited items, including cell-phones. Currently [2006] 82 of the city's public schools have permanent metal detectors installed, through which more than 100,000 students pass on their way to classes.

On April 12, five students were arrested outside of John Jay High School in Brooklyn during a walkout of over 200 against a stricter metal detector scanning policy that had resulted in the seizure of cell phones from about 80 students. According to press reports, a number of these students were manhandled and bruised by the police.

One student, Jaditza Lopez, 14, who had a large bruise on her left arm, told the *New York Daily News*, "They threw me on the ground because they thought I was protesting." Lopez spent the night in jail.

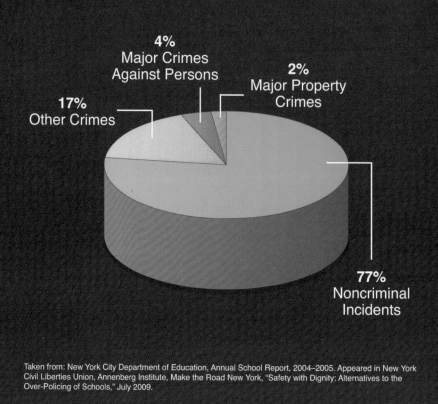

Police Involvement, by Type of Incident, in Schools with Metal Detectors

4%
Major Crimes
Against Persons

2%
Major Property
Crimes

17%
Other Crimes

77%
Noncriminal
Incidents

Taken from: New York City Department of Education, Annual School Report, 2004–2005. Appeared in New York Civil Liberties Union, Annenberg Institute, Make the Road New York, "Safety with Dignity: Alternatives to the Over-Policing of Schools," July 2009.

Another student, Maurice Reid, 16, was arrested and charged with kicking a cop. According to Reid, "She pushed me and I tried to get past her so she clubbed me." A witness told the *News*, "We were yelling at the cops to let go of the boy. He must have bruises on his legs where they hit him. I feel bad for this student. In this situation, he did nothing wrong."

Although it is located in the relatively affluent Park Slope neighborhood, John Jay's students come almost entirely from working class minority families. It is among the lowest performing schools in the city. Fewer than 4 percent of its students graduate in four years and slightly under half graduate at all. The average class size is 34 students per teacher. The school building is decaying and infested with rats and cockroaches.

Student Reaction to New Rules

Even at better performing schools, however, students have reacted with indignation at the city's intrusions into their right to privacy. In September last year, 1,500 walked out from DeWitt Clinton High School in the Bronx, with a predominately working class minority population and an 89 percent graduate rate.

The students were protesting new rules that obliged them to stand in line, often missing classes, while waiting for airport-style security checks. They were prohibited from leaving the building for lunch and subject to scrutiny by security cameras. Police confiscated pens necessary for art classes, assuming that they were used for writing graffiti.

Reacting to the imposition of random scans, Juan Antigua, one of the student leaders from Dewitt Clinton, told the *New York Times*, "It's a bad idea; just another tool that will treat us as criminals." Another Clinton student, Jessica Sosa, said, "Putting these metal detectors in deprives us of our self-esteem, of our confidence that we are going to school to learn."

New York City high school students protest the use of metal detectors in schools.

Donna Lieberman, the executive director of the New York Civil Liberties Union (NYCLU), which is examining the new policy, told the Associated Press, "This moves us closer to a surveillance society. First, we have unannounced searches in the subway. Now it's in the schools. It's a short step to unannounced searches in the street."

Police Presence in Schools

New York City has the country's largest school system, with over 1 million students and 80,000 teachers. The system is fraught with social tensions. Police presence in schools has grown, including both regular armed officers and School Safety Agents, who are uniformed employees of the Police Department but do not carry firearms. The city hired 200 more of these school officers in September, for a total of over 4,600.

A series of recent confrontations between teachers and administrators on one side and police on the other have raised the question, who is running the schools? The NYCLU filed a suit last month on behalf of two high school teachers who "were arrested, abused, and verbally harassed" by police officers in their school, according to a press release.

> **FAST FACT**
>
> In a study published in 2009, the New York Civil Liberties Union recommended to the New York City Department of Education that the installation of metal detectors in schools be discouraged.

Teachers Quinn Kronen and Cara Wolfson-Kronen were arrested at the New School for Arts and Sciences in the Longwood section of the Bronx in March 2005 after Mr. Kronen questioned the handcuffing of students following an altercation. Police yelled at Mr. Kronen and arrested Ms. Wolfson-Kronen when she objected to their behavior. She was arrested and held outside in freezing temperatures. Mr. Kronen was arrested shortly thereafter.

Stark Social Polarization

A month earlier at the Bronx Guild High School, a police officer arrested a student who had made "a loud statement in the hallway," according to NYCLU documents. The police officer, Juan Gonzalez, disrupted a class in progress to arrest the girl. When the principal, Michael [Soguero], and school aide James Burgos intervened, Gonzalez arrested them.

Gonzalez had been reported in January to the Civilian Complaint Review Board, the city's oversight board for police abuse, for allegedly placing a student in a chokehold. Incredibly, he was not reassigned. Soguero and Burgos were suspended from their jobs for over two months.

Another principal, Aurelia Curtis of Curtis High School in Staten Island, was removed from her position in December 2005 "after police complained that she had been insubstantially deferential to authority," according to another NYCLU document.

New York's educational system has come to increasingly reflect the stark social polarization that characterizes the city as a whole. The wealthiest children attend expensive private institutions while there are a few good public schools, including examination high schools, where admission is hotly contested. For the vast majority of the city's youth, however, there are the large schools that increasingly resemble holding pens and a panoply of often ill-conceived "small schools" that promise a better education but, for the most part, are unable to deliver. It is these last two categories, almost entirely consisting of working class youth, that are facing the brunt of the police repression.

EVALUATING THE AUTHOR'S ARGUMENTS:

In this viewpoint Sandy English claims that student searches erode democratic rights, mentioning the right to privacy as one of those rights. What other rights might she say are threatened by student searches?

Chapter 3

Are School Policies Aimed at Student Health Effective?

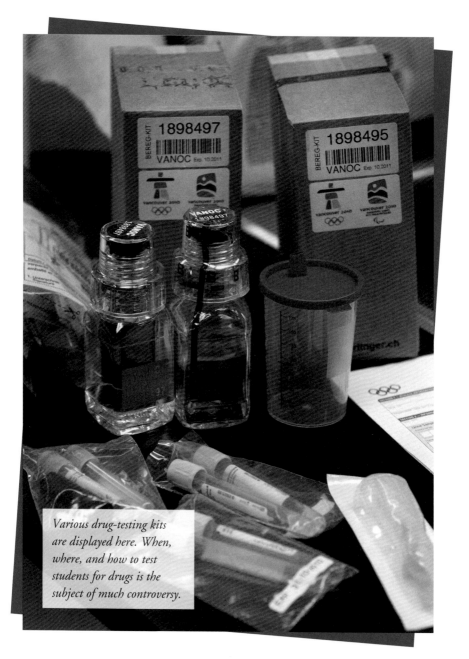

Various drug-testing kits are displayed here. When, where, and how to test students for drugs is the subject of much controversy.

Student Drug Testing Is an Effective Tool in Preventing Drug Use

Student Drug-Testing Institute

"Studies have shown drug testing to be an effective tool in preventing student drug use."

In the following viewpoint the Student Drug-Testing Institute claims that drug testing of students is one way that schools can prevent drug use and also get treatment for students who are abusing drugs. The author states that drug use is still a big problem, despite some declines in use in past years. The institute argues that because of the dangers of drug use by teens, drug testing, which is supported by law, can be an important component of drug use prevention. The Student Drug-Testing Institute was established by the US Department of Education's Office of Safe and Drug-Free Schools to provide timely information on student drug-testing programs.

AS YOU READ, CONSIDER THE FOLLOWING QUESTIONS:
1. According to the author, a study in 2006 indicated that what percentage of Americans aged twelve or older were current illicit drug users?
2. What short-term effects of drug abuse does the Student Drug-Testing Institute cite?
3. What US Supreme Court opinion does the author claim broadened the authority of public schools to test students for illegal drugs?

Random student drug testing is foremost a prevention program. Drug testing is one of several tools that schools can use as part of a comprehensive drug prevention effort. Administrators, faculty, and students at schools that conduct testing view random testing as a deterrent, and it gives students a reason to resist peer pressure to try or use drugs. Drug testing can identify students who have started using drugs so that interventions can occur early, or identify students who already have drug problems, so they can be referred for assessment, counseling, or treatment. Drug abuse not only interferes with a student's ability to learn, but it can also disrupt the teaching environment, affecting other students as well. Each school or school district that wants to start a program needs to involve the entire community in determining whether student drug testing is right for their specific situation.

Youth Drug Use

Although drug use among America's youth has declined in recent years, many young people continue to abuse harmful substances. The 2008 Monitoring the Future Survey shows that drug use among school-age youth has been in a state of decline since the 1990's; however, the proportions of 8th- and 12th-grade students indicating any use of an illicit drug in the 12 months prior to the survey showed rather modest increases since the previous year. Nearly half of 12th graders said that they have used drugs in their lifetime, and almost one third said that they use marijuana at least monthly. According to another survey conducted in 2006, an estimated 20.4 million

Americans aged 12 or older (8.3 percent of the population) were current illicit drug users, using within the past month.

Like use of other illicit drugs, steroid usage has seen a decline since usage peaked among male teens in 1999. However, steroid abuse is still a problem for many young people. The 2008 Monitoring the Future data show that 1.2 percent of 8th graders, 1.4 percent of 10th graders, and 2.5 percent of 12th graders reported using steroids at least once in their lifetime. A survey sponsored by the Centers for Disease Control and Prevention (CDC) reported that 3.9 percent of all high school students surveyed in 2007 reported use of steroid pills/shots without a doctor's prescription at some point in their lives. This figure includes 4.8 percent of 9th graders, 3.7 percent of 10th graders, 3.1 percent of 11th graders, and 3.8 percent of 12th graders.

Prescription drug abuse is also high and is increasing. The 2008 Monitoring the Future data indicate that 15.4 percent of 12th

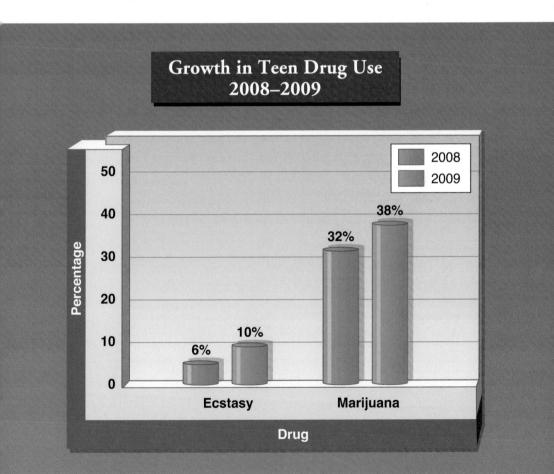

Growth in Teen Drug Use 2008–2009

Taken from: Partnership for a Drug-Free America/MetLife Foundation, "2009 Partnership/MetLife Foundation Attitude Tracking Study," 2010.

graders reported using a prescription drug nonmedically within the past year. Vicodin, an opiate pain reliever, continues to be abused at unacceptably high levels. Many of the drugs used by 12th graders are prescription drugs or, in the case of cough medicine, are available over the counter.

Despite some declines in drug use, much remains to be done. Youth still face a barrage of media messages and peer pressure that promote drug use. Random student drug-testing programs are effective prevention strategies to help adolescents refuse drugs, when offered.

Student Drug Testing

Communities first need to identify their drug problems. This becomes the basis of developing a consensus for student drug testing. Schools must first determine whether there is a need for testing. Such a need can be determined from student drug-use surveys, reports by teachers and other school staff about student drug use, reports about drug use from parents and others in the community, and from discoveries of drugs, drug paraphernalia, or residues at school.

> ## FAST FACT
>
> Many schools receive federal money from the Office of Safe and Drug-Free Schools in the US Department of Education to pay for student drug-testing programs.

Drug testing should never be undertaken as a stand-alone response to a drug problem. If testing is done, it should be one component of a comprehensive prevention and intervention program in compliance with local, state, and federal laws, with the common goal of reducing students' use of illegal drugs and misuse of prescription drugs.

Drug use can turn into abuse and then into addiction, trapping users in a vicious cycle that can ruin lives and destroy families. Studies have shown drug testing to be an effective tool in preventing student drug use. The expectation that they may be randomly tested is enough to make some students stop using drugs—or never start in the first place. School-based drug testing is also an excellent tool for getting students who use drugs the help they need.

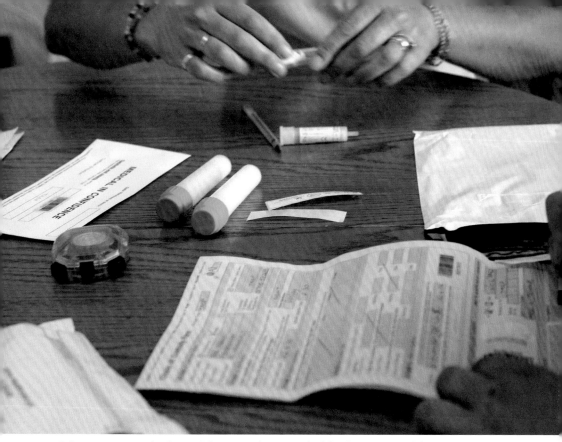

A drug-testing sample obtained from a student is readied for shipment to a laboratory.

The Dangers of Drug Use

According to the 2007 National Survey on Drug Use and Health students who use drugs are statistically more likely to drop out of school, bring guns to school, steal, and be involved in fighting or other delinquent behavior. Drug abuse not only interferes with a student's ability to learn, it also disrupts the orderly environment necessary for all students to succeed. Obviously, reducing the likelihood of these disruptive behaviors benefits everyone involved in a school environment.

Teens are especially vulnerable to drug abuse when the brain and body are still developing. Most teens do not use drugs, but for those that do, it can lead to a wide range of adverse effects on the brain, the body, behavior, and health.

Short term: Even a single use of an intoxicating drug can affect a person's judgment and decision-making—resulting in accidents, poor performance in a school or sports activity, unplanned risky behavior, and the risk of overdosing.

Long term: Repeated drug abuse can lead to serious problems, such as poor academic outcomes, mood changes (depending on the drug: depression, anxiety, paranoia, psychosis), and social or family problems caused or worsened by drugs. Repeated drug use can also lead to the disease of addiction. Studies show that the earlier a teen begins using drugs, the more likely he or she will develop a substance abuse problem or addiction. Conversely, if teens stay away from drugs while in high school, they are less likely to develop a substance abuse problem later in life.

The Research About Random Drug Testing

There is not very much research in this area and early research shows mixed results. A study published in 2007 found that student athletes who participated in randomized drug testing had overall rates of drug use similar to students who did not take part in the program, and in fact, some indicators of future drug abuse increased among those participating in the drug-testing program.

In another study, Hunterdon Central Regional High School in New Jersey saw significant reductions in 20 of 28 drug use categories after 2 years of a drug-testing program (e.g., cocaine use by seniors dropped from 13 percent to 4 percent). A third study, from Ball State University, showed that 73 percent of high school principals reported a reduction in drug use among students subjected to a drug-testing policy, but only 2 percent reported an increase. Because of the limited number of studies on this topic, more research is warranted. . . .

Drug Testing and the Law

The federal government recognizes drug testing as one tool that local schools can choose as a component of a broad drug prevention effort. Each school or school district that wants to start a program needs to involve the entire community in determining whether student drug testing is right for their specific situation.

The Supreme Court of the United States first determined that drug testing of student athletes is constitutional in a June 1995 decision. Voting 6 to 3 in *Vernonia School District [47J] v. Acton,* the court upheld the constitutionality of a policy requiring student athletes to submit to random drug testing.

In June 2002, the U.S. Supreme Court broadened the authority of public schools to test students for illegal drugs. Voting 5 to 4 in *Pottawatomie County v. Earls*, the court ruled to allow random drug tests for all middle and high school students participating in competitive extracurricular activities. The ruling greatly expanded the scope of school drug testing.

EVALUATING THE AUTHOR'S ARGUMENTS:

In this viewpoint the Student Drug-Testing Institute says that drug testing is an effective tool in preventing drug use. Do you agree with this claim? Defend your answer.

"Even if drug testing is done randomly and without suspicion, it's not associated with a change in the number of students who use drugs in any category."

Student Drug Testing Is Not an Effective Tool in Preventing Drug Use

Ryan Grim

In the following viewpoint Ryan Grim argues that student drug testing does not prevent drug use. Grim contends that two different studies have shown that student drug testing, including random testing, is not effective. He claims that the practice of student drug testing by the government has continued nonetheless, pushed in part by the drug-testing industry, which stands to gain much by increased testing of students. Grim is senior congressional correspondent for the *Huffington Post* and author of *This Is Your Country on Drugs: The Secret History of Getting High in America.*

AS YOU READ, CONSIDER THE FOLLOWING QUESTIONS:

1. Grim claims that a 2003 study compared the rates of drug use at a school that tested for drugs with one that did not test, finding what?
2. Did the White House's Program Assessment Rating Tool determine that the Safe and Drug Free Schools State Grants program was a success or a failure, according to the author?
3. The author claims that the drug-testing industry makes what amount of money annually?

D
rug testing of the American public has been steadily broadening over the past 20 years, from soldiers to grocery baggers to high-school and middle-school students. In its 2007 budget, the Bush administration asks for $15 million to fund random drug testing of students—if approved, a 50 percent increase over 2006. Officials from the federal drug czar's office are crisscrossing the country to sell the testing to school districts.

Yet, according to the two major studies that have been conducted on student testing, it doesn't actually reduce drug use. "Of most importance, drug testing still is found not to be associated with students' reported illicit drug use—even random testing that potentially subjects the entire student body," determined the authors of the most recent study.

It seems like common sense that if students are warned they could be caught getting high any day in school, they'd be less likely to risk it. And principals and the drug czar's office argue that this random chance "gives kids a reason to say no." But teens are notorious for assuming that nothing bad will happen to them. *Sure, some people get caught, but not me.* In addition, a student who chooses to do drugs already has more than a random chance of getting caught—adults are everywhere in this world.

Someone could see her, smell smoke, see her bloodshot eyes, or wonder what the hell is so funny. And since most schools test only students who do something more than just show up for class—like

Estimated Increase in Student Drug Testing

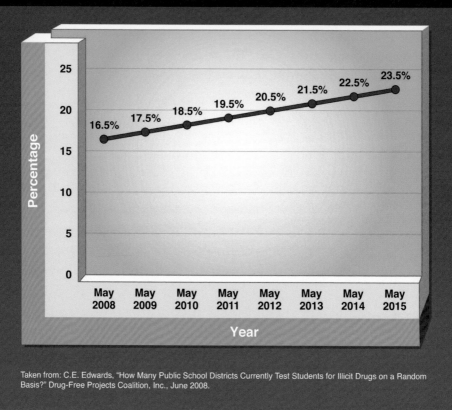

Estimated Percentage of US Public School Districts with Random Student Drug-Testing Programs

Taken from: C.E. Edwards, "How Many Public School Districts Currently Test Students for Illicit Drugs on a Random Basis?" Drug-Free Projects Coalition, Inc., June 2008.

join an after-school club, park on campus, or play a sport—kids can avoid the activities rather than quit puffing. Testing may not change much more of the equation than that.

Such are the findings of two major studies. The first study, published in early 2003, looked at 76,000 students in eighth, 10th, and 12th grades in hundreds of schools, between the years 1998 and 2001. It was conducted by Ryoko Yamaguchi, Lloyd Johnston, and Patrick O'Malley out of the University of Michigan, which also produces Monitoring the Future, the university's highly regarded annual survey of student drug use, which is funded by the National Institute on Drug Abuse and whose numbers the White House regularly cites.

The early 2003 Michigan study compared the rates of drug use, as measured by Monitoring the Future, in schools that did some type of drug testing to schools that did not. The researchers controlled for various demographic differences and found across the board that drug testing was ineffective; there was no statistically significant difference in the number of users at a school that tested for drugs and a similar school that didn't.

The White House criticized the Michigan study for failing to look at the efficacy of random testing. So, Yamaguchi, Johnston, and O'Malley added the random element and ran their study again, this time adding data for the year 2002. The follow-up study, published later in 2003, tracked 94,000 middle-and high-school students. It reached the same results as its precursor. Even if drug testing is done randomly and without suspicion, it's not associated with a change in the number of students who use drugs in any category. The Michigan follow-up found one exception: In schools that randomly tested students, 12th-graders were *more* likely to smoke marijuana.

Results like these would mean budget cuts or death for some government programs. The White House has devised its own rating system, known as the Program Assessment Rating Tool, to help it cull failed initiatives. (These generally turn out to be the type of programs you wouldn't expect a Republican administration to like, but that's another story.) In 2002, PART deemed "ineffective" the Safe and Drug Free Schools State Grants program, the umbrella for school drug testing. The Office of Management and Budget, which runs the PART evaluations, writes on its Web site, "The program has failed to demonstrate effectiveness in reducing youth drug use, violence, and crime." The PART evaluation did not single out drug testing, which is a small part of the overall state grants program. Still, combined with the Michigan studies, what we have here is a bureaucratic pounding. That hasn't stopped President Bush from sounding an upbeat note. In his 2004 State of the Union, he said, "I proposed new funding to continue our

> **FAST FACT**
>
> Marijuana is the top drug identified in drug tests and the drug with one of the longest detection periods in the body after use.

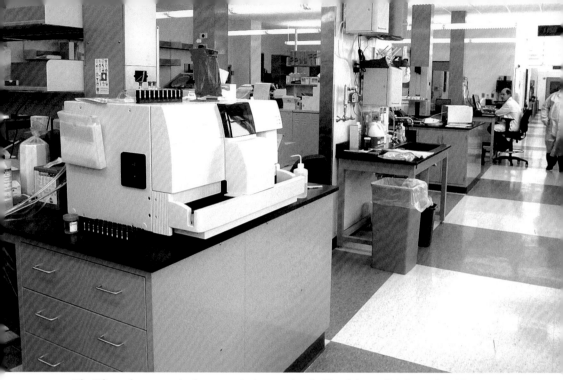

The Pfizer pharmaceutical company's drug-testing facility (pictured) is located in New Haven, Connecticut. The drug-testing industry generates about $766 million a year in revenue for pharmaceutical companies.

aggressive, community-based strategy to reduce demand for illegal drugs. Drug testing in our schools has proven to be an effective part of this effort."

Pressed for evidence to support the administration's bid to increase funds for testing, drug officials challenge the Michigan study's methodology. Drug czar John Walters has called for "detailed pre- and post-random testing data"—that is, a study of the rate of drug use at a school before a random testing program was initiated and then again afterward. Such a study is currently under way with federal funds, but it comes with a built-in flaw. Drug-use rates are obtained in questionnaires that school administrators give to students. If the administrators are asking students about their drug-use habits while they have the power to randomly test them, how honest can we expect the students to be, no matter what anonymity they're promised?

Like Walters, the $766 million drug-testing industry isn't ready to give up on testing students, for which it charges between $14 and $30 a cupful of pee. Melissa Moskal, executive director of the 1,300-member

Drug and Alcohol Testing Industry Association, pointed me to a preliminary study that she likes better than Michigan's and that Walters also frequently references. The study is funded by the Department of Education and produced by the Institute for Behavior and Health, and its lead author is Robert DuPont, a former White House drug official. DuPont is also a partner at Bensinger, DuPont & Associates (BDA). DuPont says that Bensinger "doesn't have anything to do with drug testing." But the company's Web site states: "BDA offers a range of products designed to help employers establish and manage workplace drug and alcohol testing programs."

DuPont's study, which he calls "descriptive," chose nine schools that met certain criteria, the first of which was, "The student drug testing program's apparent success." The study's methodology appears to add to the slant. Rather than gathering information from students and analyzing it, DuPont relies on a questionnaire that asks how effective administrators think their random drug-testing program is. He doesn't claim neutrality. "I can't quite get the argument that [drug testing] wouldn't work," he says. He's now working on an evaluation of eight schools. The results won't be ready soon, but let's venture a prediction: Random drug testing will come out looking good.

EVALUATING THE AUTHORS' ARGUMENTS:

In this viewpoint Ryan Grim claims that two studies have shown the ineffectiveness of student drug testing. In what specific ways do you think Grim would criticize the claims of the Student Drug-Testing Institute, author of the previous viewpoint?

Schools Should Ban Junk Food

Inez Russell

In the following viewpoint Inez Russell contends that junk food in schools is a real danger for kids. She argues that parents need to control what kids eat, but when kids are away from home parents are not able to control their eating habits. New rules about what kids can buy in school are a start, Russell contends, but she concludes that they do not go far enough and believes that all high-calorie snacks should be eliminated from schools. Russell is the editor of specialty magazines at *The Santa Fe New Mexican,* a daily newspaper in New Mexico.

"Dump the vending machines altogether."

AS YOU READ, CONSIDER THE FOLLOWING QUESTIONS:

1. Russell's concern about junk good in schools is driven by a concern about what?
2. The author wants to be able to send her child to school knowing that he will not be able to do what?
3. What does Russell suggest as a solution to parent and school worries about junk food in schools?

S ending your kid off to school is scary for parents. Whether you're worried about bullies, the quality of teaching, traffic or any of the many real (or not-so-real) fears we modern parents tend to obsess over, there's always a shadow in the back of our minds that our kids aren't safe without us.

Junk Food in School

With all that to worry about, we shouldn't have to worry that going to school will help make our kids fat (or sick).

That's why I support schools getting out of the business of helping Big Food push chemically treated, sugared, salted and otherwise bad food and drinks on children.

I was pleased to read the stories that New Mexico public schools are tightening the screws on what kinds of drinks and foods can be sold in our schools.

After all, we are in the midst of a nationwide obesity crisis—among both children and adults. But it's the health of children that concerns me. We as a nation face the real possibility that children alive today

US Senator Tom Harkin speaks at a press conference about bipartisan legislation that will force schools to serve healthier foods than the junk food displayed here.

will have shorter life spans than their parents because they eat too many calories. Junk food could kill our kids.

And yet as a society we sit back and let Big Food sell that junk to our kids, defending it as a "free choice." We don't adopt the common-sense solutions of regulating TV advertising of junk to kids or taxing low-nutrition, high-calorie foods or even offering tax breaks to companies that make great food kids want to eat.

Away from Parents

It's up to parents to make sure their kids eat right, the thinking goes. It is up to parents, and as a parent, I make sure my son eats plenty of vegetables, good fats, protein and fruits. At home.

> **FAST FACT**
>
> The average twelve-ounce can of soda has about one hundred fifty calories, all of which come from sugar, with each can of soda containing forty grams of sugar—the equivalent of about ten sugar cubes.

Away from home, I'm not there all the time, and I would like some help. I would like to be able to send my kid to school with a dollar, knowing that he can't buy a 200-calorie (or higher) drink out of a vending machine.

I don't care if the drink has carbonation or not. I just don't want that many calories—whether from sugary juice or one of those nasty sports drinks—available.

And, since I can't go to school with him every day, I keep money out of his way. Because when everyone else is chugging a lemonade, there's little chance my son will just buy water.

And those are calories he, and so many other children, can't afford.

New Rules a Start

Next year [2007], rules from the state Public Education Department well help parents who worry about nutrition. In elementary schools, only 2-percent milk, soy milk or water will be permitted. Extra food for fundraisers won't be allowed during school hours under the guidelines. At middle and high school, fruit juice can be sold, but the state wants to limit the drinks to 125 calories per container. Some fund-raising foods can be sold at the middle- and high-school level, but the state is limiting the number of calories and fat and sugar grams.

Those guidelines will be a great help.

Unfortunately, additives in drinks still make the vending machines a scary proposition. There's the controversy over artificial sweeteners. Now we find out that some drinks, such as Diet Pepsi Wild Cherry, Hawaiian Punch and Tropicana Lemonade, might contain too high a concentration of benzene, which has been linked to cancer. The state is still studying this potential health threat.

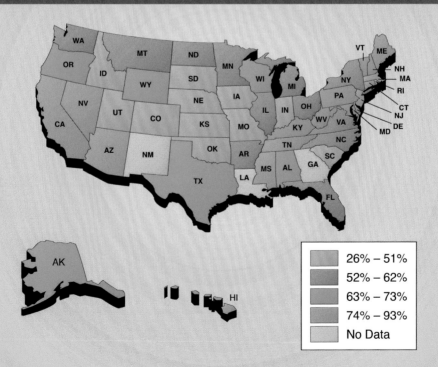

Limits on Fruit Beverages Available to Students in Secondary Schools

Percentage of secondary schools in which students cannot purchase soda pop or fruit drinks that are not 100 percent juice from vending machines or at the school store, canteen, or snack bar.

- 26% – 51%
- 52% – 62%
- 63% – 73%
- 74% – 93%
- No Data

Taken from: Centers for Disease Control and Prevention, *School Health Profiles 2008: Characteristics of Health Programs Among Secondary Schools*. Atlanta, GA: US Department of Health and Human Services, CDC: 2009.

This is just one mom's opinion, but I have a simple solution, a way to save countless staff hours of research and help parents rest easy. Dump the vending machines altogether. That way, schools can worry about educating kids. We parents will take care of feeding them.

And, if kids get thirsty at school, let them take a walk—to the water fountain.

EVALUATING THE AUTHOR'S ARGUMENTS:

In this viewpoint Inez Russell contends that "Big Food" is allowed in schools because people defend it as a free choice. Do you believe this is a valid reason to allow any type of food or drink in school? Defend your answer.

Viewpoint

4

A Ban on Junk Food and Marketing Will Not End Childhood Obesity

Pierce Hollingsworth

"The current rush to ban junk foods is a misguided— maybe even tragic—exercise in shallow political correctness and gross ineffectiveness."

In the following viewpoint Pierce Hollingsworth argues that junk food is being blamed for problems caused by bad habits. He claims that the recent move toward banning junk food is a misguided policy and that the real solution to childhood obesity lies elsewhere. Hollingsworth contends that it is not food marketing and the presence of certain foods in schools that are to blame for a rise in obesity but rather the sedentary lifestyles of today's children. Hollingsworth is vice president of Stagnito Media, a publishing company, and adjunct instructor at the Medill School of Journalism at Northwestern University in Evanston, Illinois.

AS YOU READ, CONSIDER THE FOLLOWING QUESTIONS:
1. The author claims that food and the food industry are far easier to demonize than what?
2. Hollingsworth says that the Institute of Medicine claimed the leading cause of childhood obesity was what?
3. The author cites what four causes of the rise in obesity among all age groups?

E ngland: "A ban on confectionery, crisps and fizzy drinks being provided in schools looks certain to begin in September following the publication of advice to ministers by the new School Food Trust yesterday" (*Guardian Newspapers*, March 3, 2006).

United States: "Congress wants to expel all bad food from the nation's schools" (*Detroit News*, April 7, 2006).

The Food Is Not the Problem

Bad food or bad habits? Obesity is a well documented, nagging and very real public health problem—not just in the United States, but throughout most of the industrialized world. If we all ate from a limited menu, and if a few of those menu items were solely responsible for making us fat, then it would be easy to simply cut them from the menu or limit their availability. Or if certain foods were truly physically addictive and caused us to fatten up, much like cigarettes cause cancer, then banning them would be a no-brainer. But that's not the case.

The current rush to ban junk foods is a misguided—maybe even tragic—exercise in shallow political correctness and gross ineffectiveness. Efforts by the food industry, responsible public policy groups and trade associations to formulate more effective tactics appear to be too little, too late. Nevertheless, a coordinated long-term effort by the food industry is essential. There is no quick fix.

Make no mistake, food and the food industry are far easier to demonize, regulate and litigate than a culture of laziness and indulgence. It's less complicated to assert that kids are fat because they're victims of clever food marketing than to lay the blame on parents and schools not teaching personal responsibility and good habits, or requiring sufficient physical exercise.

The Focus on the Food Industry

This column has periodically addressed the rising tide of litigation and regulation slowly oozing into the marketplace—and warned that the trend will not only continue, but intensify. To that end, schools have become the battleground. They're the current hub around which the blame battle revolves.

In May [2006], the Federal Trade Commission [FTC] and the Department of Health and Human Services released a report recommending concrete steps that the food industry should take to change marketing "and other practices" to make progress against childhood obesity. The press release that accompanied the report was telling. It

Parents' Opinions About Their Overweight Children

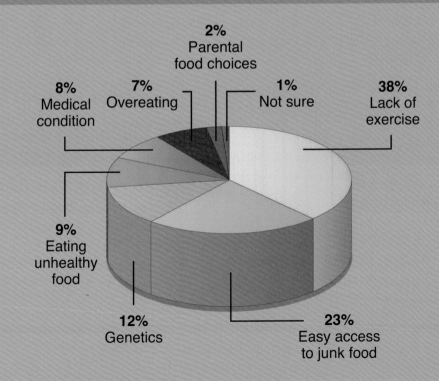

Which ONE of the following factors would you say is the most important in contributing to your child being overweight?

2%
Parental food choices

8%
Medical condition

7%
Overeating

1%
Not sure

38%
Lack of exercise

9%
Eating unhealthy food

12%
Genetics

23%
Easy access to junk food

Taken from: Associated Press/America Online Poll, October 5–23, 2005.

noted, in part: "[Report] participants acknowledged that many factors contribute to childhood obesity, but recognized that regardless of the causes, responsible marketing can play a positive role in improving children's diets and exercise behavior."

According to FTC Chairman Deborah Platt Majoras, "Responsible industry-generated action and effective self-regulation are critical to addressing the national problem of childhood obesity. The FTC plans to monitor industry efforts closely, and we expect to see real improvements."

She's not alone. Over the past several months, the food industry has been hammered by condemning studies and recommendations. Last December, the Institute of Medicine [IOM] singled out food marketing as the leading cause of childhood obesity and called for government intervention. "If the industries' voluntary efforts fail to shift the emphasis of television advertising to healthier products aimed at children, then the [IOM] committee recommends that Congress pursue legislation," stated Dr. Michael McGinnis, the report chair.

And most recently, in June, a Washington, D.C., delegate to the U.S. House, (Dem.) Eleanor Holmes Norton, introduced a bill to restore the FTC's authority to regulate marketing to children under the age of 18, because junk food advertising is "urging our kids to eat themselves into bad health."

> ## FAST FACT
>
> In 2010 the Barack Obama Administration launched a nationwide campaign called "Let's Move," which has four key initiatives: informing parents about nutrition and exercise; improving the quality of food in schools; making health foods affordable; and focusing on physical education.

The Real Problem

The problem is that kids now spend more time on the Internet and listening to iPods than they do watching TV. In fact, studies show that the current kid generation is the first to truly multi-task—able to watch, type, communicate, play video games and listen to different media stimuli at the same time. This may not make them smarter or healthier, but they can do it.

An opponent of junk food bans, the author maintains that such foods are not the major contributor to childhood obesity. Instead, he points to a sedentary population that values hours spent on the Internet more than exercise and other physical activity.

No doubt marketing plays a role in influencing human behavior, particularly in a media-sopped culture. But the over emphasis on food advertising is a troubling waste of time. Kids are getting fatter, yet the FTC found that they see "significantly" fewer ads on television today than 28 years ago. As of last year, the average number of ads totaled 13 per day, versus 18 in 1977. A University of Chicago PhD candidate, Fernando Wilson, recently released data that shows kids' TV viewing actually in decline over that past 25 years—while inactivity has been on the rise.

Consider this:

If all but fresh fruits and vegetables were eliminated from school foodservice and television advertising, and if the government went one step further and placed quotas on calories and fat contained in fast food meals, would the childhood obesity epidemic be stemmed?

Of course not. Obesity is up in all age groups because of the low cost of food, wide 24/7 availability, sedentary lifestyles, and less stigma attached to being overweight. Yet food and the industry that manufactures and sells it are in the litigious/legislative cross-hairs. It's the politically expedient quick fix, unfortunately our kids will just continue to get fatter—with or without junk food. The food industry will do well to continue to support rational public policy and directly support efforts to promote exercise and healthy eating habits.

EVALUATING THE AUTHORS' ARGUMENTS:

In this viewpoint Pierce Hollingsworth claims that parents and schools should teach good habits or require more exercise rather than ban junk food or junk food marketing. How do you think Inez Russell, author of the previous viewpoint, would respond to his contentions?

Abstinence-Only Education Programs Are Effective

Rebecca Hagelin

"Our teens deserve better than just a condom and a message to 'be safe.'"

In the following viewpoint Rebecca Hagelin argues that abstinence-only programs for sex education have been unfairly criticized. She claims that real teens and facts dispute the critics' claim that abstinence-only programs do not work. In fact, Hagelin says, such programs have caused a decrease in the number of teens who become sexually active in high school. Hagelin is vice president of communications and marketing for the Heritage Foundation, a conservative public policy research organization, and author of *Home Invasion: Protecting Your Family in a Culture That's Gone Stark Raving Mad.*

AS YOU READ, CONSIDER THE FOLLOWING QUESTIONS:

1. The author claims that critics of abstinence-only programs resort to what argument in support of their view?
2. According to the research Hagelin cites, what fraction of teenagers has engaged in sexual activity?
3. Hagelin claims that the rise in what three things shows that comprehensive sex education is not working?

Who could argue with the idea that, when it comes to sex education, our teenagers should be taught to say "no"? Considering what's at stake (their health, their future, their dignity as human beings, their morality)—and because we love them and want what's best for them—nothing short of a clear-cut abstinence message will do.

Critics of Abstinence-Only Programs

At least, that's how it appears out here in the Real World. In the rarified air of a congressional hearing room, it's another matter. According to several witnesses (including John Santelli of the Guttmacher Institute and Max Siegel of the AIDS Alliance for Children, Youth & Families) who spoke recently [2008] before the House Committee on Oversight and Government Reform, abstinence education is not only impractical, it's dangerous.

Many critics of the abstinence-only programs that have been federally funded over the past 11 years resort to the old kids-will-be-kids argument. They'll "do it anyway," we're told, so we're wasting time and money on an idealistic charade. Worse, we're depriving our rutting youth of the "protection" they need to make their unions non-fruitful and disease-free.

> **FAST FACT**
>
> The first virginity pledge program, True Love Waits, was launched in 1993 by the Southern Baptist Convention.

Lawmakers didn't hear from actual teenagers, though. "The greatest failure of this committee was not allowing those that were being talked about—the teens themselves—the opportunity to share how and why abstinence programs have worked for them," said Leslee Unruh, president of the Abstinence Clearinghouse. "I saw abstinent young adults in the audience appearing frustrated, saying they wish they could share their opinion on this matter."

A quick review of the resulting coverage finds that the witnesses' agenda has a receptive audience among the media. Typical headlines include "Abstinence-only sex ed discredited" (*Fort Wayne Journal Gazette*, Indiana), "A real-world solution to teenage pregnancy"

(*Houston Chronicle*) and "Abstinence-only education not enough" (*Rapid City Journal*, South Dakota).

The Actual Research

I hate to interrupt their collective dream with something as inconvenient as the facts. Actual research, however, shows that the abstinence message works.

In a major new paper, Christine Kim and Robert Rector of The Heritage Foundation sifted carefully through numerous studies on the effectiveness of abstinence programs and found clear evidence that they work. "In addition to teaching the benefits of abstaining from sexual activity until marriage, abstinence programs focus on developing character traits that prepare youths for future-oriented goals," the researchers write.

Those Thinking Sexual Abstinence Programs Are Effective, by Age

"Do you think these programs to promote abstinence have been effective, somewhat effective, not very effective, or not at all effective in preventing or reducing . . . ?"

	Age					
	18–24	25–29	30–39	40–49	50–64	65+
	n=148	n=129	n=206	n=457	n=586	n=435
	Percentage Saying Somewhat or Very Effective					
HIV/AIDS	56	60	43	41	37	31
Unwanted Pregnancies	49	52	35	33	28	30
Extramarital Sex	28	31	22	22	19	18

Taken from: The Harris Poll, December 8 and 14, 2005.

But some teenagers get pregnant anyway, the critics reply. True. As Kim and Rector note:

> Each year, 2.6 million teenagers become sexually active—a rate of 7,000 teens per day. Among high school students, nearly half report having engaged in sexual activity, and one-third are currently active.

Yet this doesn't amount to an argument *against* teaching abstinence. No one ever said that abstinence programs would wipe out teen pregnancy. Any improvement on this front is nothing short of miraculous, given the barrage of trashy media and cultural messages targeted at kids. The critics are engaging in a classic "straw man" argument, and they should be called on it.

The real question is: Do abstinence programs make the problem any better? Kim and Rector show that they do. In my book, *Home Invasion*, I cited additional Heritage research:

> In the decade or so that true abstinence-only programs have grown in popularity, the percentage of teens who say they have had sex by the time they leave high school has fallen from 56 to 48. A popular component of the abstinence-only movement, virginity pledges, has produced even better results. According to The Heritage Foundation, teens who take a virginity pledge are less likely to become pregnant by age 18, and will have fewer sexual partners in their lifetime than teens who do not take a pledge.

The Failure of Comprehensive Sex Ed

We also must ask ourselves if the alternative—so-called "comprehensive sex education," with its pornographic emphasis on the mechanics of sex—is any better. These programs have proven to be dismal failures. They've held sway for years in our nation's classrooms, and teen sexual behavior, STDs and pregnancies have all been going up. As Kim and Rector point out:

> Today's young people face strong peer pressure to engage in risky behavior and must navigate media and popular culture

Abstinence programs like the "Purity Ring Ceremony," in which teens pledge to refrain from sex until marriage, have been highly touted by the religious right.

that endorse and even glamorize permissiveness and casual sex. Alarmingly, the government implicitly supports these messages by spending over $1 billion each year promoting contraception and safe-sex education—12 times what it spends on abstinence education.

I hope you find that as outrageous as I do. Our teens deserve better than just a condom and a message to "be safe." Our children are not animals, incapable of controlling themselves. They are not hopelessly immoral creatures who are going to "do it anyway." Yet "comprehensive" sex ed teaches them that they're just that. Parents, this is a slander against our youth. It's a lie—one that we must fight.

Teaching abstinence may be hard work—and heaven knows it's not going to win you any popularity contests. But for the sake of our teens, there's simply no substitute. In the end, you're the only real "protection" they've got. So don't let them down.

Abstinence-Only Education Programs Are Not Effective

Ellen Goodman

"All in all, abstinence-only education has become emblematic of the rule of ideology over science."

In the following viewpoint Ellen Goodman claims that measuring the success of abstinence-only sex education by counting the number of teens who take abstinence pledges is deeply flawed. In fact, Goodman argues, most of those who take the pledge break it. She laments the amount of funding poured into abstinence-only programs over the years and calls for evidence-based programs to be employed in the future. Goodman is an author, commentator, and columnist, whose column appeared regularly in *The Boston Globe* for many years prior to her 2010 retirement.

AS YOU READ, CONSIDER THE FOLLOWING QUESTIONS:

1. Goodman says that a study by researcher Janet Rosenbaum showed what about the effectiveness of abstinence pledges?
2. The author claims that funding for abstinence-only education increased by how much between 2001 and 2008?
3. The author claims that how many teenage girls will get pregnant in 2009?

I hate to bring this up right now when the ink is barely dry on your New Year's resolution. But if history is any guide, you are likely to fall off the assorted wagons to which you are currently lashed.

I don't say this to disparage your will power. Hang onto that celery stick for dear life. And even if you stop doing those stomach crunches and start sneaking out for a smoke, at least you can comfort yourself with fond memories of your moment of resolution.

Compare that to the factoid in the newest research about teens who pledge abstinence. The majority not only break the pledge, they forget they ever made it.

This study of about 1,000 teens comes from Johns Hopkins researcher Janet Rosenbaum, who compared teens who took a pledge of abstinence with teens of similar backgrounds and beliefs who didn't. She found absolutely no difference in their sexual behavior, or the age at which they began having sex, or the number of their partners.

FAST FACT

For the 2010 federal budget, the Barack Obama administration eliminated more than $170 million in funding targeted at abstinence programs.

In fact, the only difference was that the group that promised to remain abstinent was significantly less likely to use birth control, especially condoms, when they did have sex. The lesson many students seemed to retain from their abstinence-only program was a negative and inaccurate view of contraception.

This is not just a primer on the capacity for teenage denial or the inner workings of adolescent neurobiology. What makes this study important is this: "virginity pledges" are one of the ways that the government measures whether abstinence-only education is "working." They count the pledges as proof that teens will abstain. It turns out that this is like counting New Year's resolutions as proof that you lost 10 pounds.

We have been here before. And before that. And before that.

When he was running for president, Bush promised, "My administration will elevate abstinence education from an afterthought to an

Many opponents of abstinence-only policies point out that although $1.5 billion has been spent on such programs, there are no studies proving that they are effective.

urgent goal." Over the last eight years, a cottage industry of "abstinence-only until marriage" purveyors became a McMansion industry. Funding increased from $73 million a year in 2001 to $204 million in 2008. That's a total of $1.5 billion in federal money for an ideology in search of a methodology. And half the states refused funds to pay for sex mis-education.

"Teen Girls and STD," cartoon by Mike Keefe, *The Denver Post*, www.CagleCartoons.com. Copyright © by Mike Keefe and CagleCartoons.com. All rights reserved.

By now, there's an archive of research showing that the binge was a bust. Programs mandated to teach only "the social, psychological and health gains (of) abstaining from sexual activity" and to warn of the dangers of having sex have been awarded failing grades for truth and effectiveness. As Rosenbaum says, "Abstinence-only education is required to give inaccurate information. Teens are savvy consumers of information and know what they are getting."

Our investment in abstinence-only may not be a scam on the scale of Bernie Madoff. But this industry has had standards for truth as loose as some mortgage lenders. All in all, abstinence-only education has become emblematic of the rule of ideology over science.

The sorry part is that sex education got caught in the culture wars. It's been framed, says Bill Alberts of the National Campaign to Prevent Teen Pregnancy, as a battle between "those who wanted virginity pledges and those who wanted to hand out condoms to 14-year-olds."

Meanwhile, six in 10 teens have sex before they leave high school and 730,000 teenage girls will get pregnant this year. We see them everywhere from "Juno" to Juneau—or to be more accurate, Anchorage, where Sarah Palin, advocate of abstinence-only education, just became an unplanned grandparent.

What the overwhelming majority of protective parents actually want is not a political battle. They want teens to delay sex and to have honest information about sexuality, including contraception. The programs that work best combine those lessons.

Soon Congress and the new administration will be anteing up annual funding for abstinence-only programs. As Cecile Richards of Planned Parenthood says, abstinence-only education was "an experiment gone awry. We spent $1.5 billion and can't point to a single study that says this helps. If it doesn't help, why fund it?"

Teens are not the only masters of denial. But we are finally stepping back from the culture wars. We are, with luck, returning to something that used to be redundant—evidence-based science. That's a pledge worth signing . . . and remembering.

EVALUATING THE AUTHORS' ARGUMENTS:

In this viewpoint Ellen Goodman claims that abstinence-only education not only fails at keeping teens abstinent but leaves them more likely to forego contraception when they do have sex. If true, does this support favoring comprehensive sex education over abstinence-only education? How would Rebecca Hagelin, author of the previous viewpoint, respond?

Facts About School Policies

Editor's note: These facts can be used in reports to add credibility when making important points or claims.

School Policies Limiting Student Expression

According to the National Center for Education Statistics, during the 2007–2008 school year:
- Fifty-five percent of schools enforced a strict dress code.
- Eighteen percent of schools required students to wear uniforms.

Student Opinion About School Policies Limiting Student Expression

According to a 2005 Gallup Poll of students aged 13 to 17 on public school policies:
- Seventy-five percent thought schools should be allowed to restrict foul language in writing assignments.
- Forty-five percent thought schools should be allowed to restrict what students write in the school newspaper.
- Forty-four percent thought schools should be allowed to ban books, newspapers, and magazines.

School Security Policies at Public Schools

According to the National Center for Education Statistics, during the 2007–2008 school year:
- Ninety-nine percent of schools required visitors to sign in or check in.
- Ninety percent of schools had locked or monitored doors on school buildings;
- Forty-three percent of schools had locked or monitored gates on school grounds;
- Sixty-five percent of schools closed the campus for most students during lunch;
- Fifty-five percent of schools used security cameras to monitor the school.
- Eleven percent of schools performed random sweeps for contraband.

- Fve percent of schools performed random metal detector checks on students.

Concern Among Parents and Children About School Safety

According to a 2006 Gallup Poll:
- Twenty-five percent of parents said that they were fearful for their child's safety, down from 47 percent in 1999 just after the Columbine High School shooting in Littleton, Colorado.
- Eleven percent of parents said that their child was concerned about his or her safety.

Drug Policies at Public Schools

According to the National Center for Education Statistics, during the 2007–2008 school year:
- Ninety-one percent of schools prohibited all tobacco use on school grounds.
- Six percent of schools tested athletes for drugs.
- Five percent of schools tested students in extracurricular activities (other than athletes) for drugs.

Students and Sex Education Policies

According to a 2005 Gallup Poll of students aged 13 to 17:
- Sixty-four percent of students have taken a sex education course at school.
- Sixty-one percent of those said their school took a safe-sex approach to sex education, whereas 36 percent said their school took an abstinence-only approach.

According to a 2005 Pew Research Center poll:
- Seventy-eight percent of adults favor allowing public schools to provide students with birth control information, but 76 percent also believe that schools should teach teenagers to abstain from sex until marriage.
- Among parents, 7 percent think public schools are doing an excellent job with sex education, 31 percent a good job, 28 percent a fair job, 19 percent a poor job, and 15 percent do not know.

School Cafeterias

According to a 2007 Gallup Poll:
- Twenty-one percent of parents believe that lunches served at school are very nutritious.

- Forty-two percent of parents believe that lunches served at school are somewhat nutritious.
- Seventeen percent of parents believe that lunches served at school are not very nutritious.
- Ten percent of parents believe that lunches served at school are not at all nutritious.
- Forty-three percent of parents believe their child's school is offering too many foods that should not be served to children, but 48 percent believe the school is not offering too many objectionable foods.
- Sixty-six percent of parents believe that the school should offer more fruits, vegetables, and whole grains.
- Nine percent of parents believe that school lunches are a great deal to blame for childhood obesity, whereas 30 percent believe that school lunches are not at all to blame.

Organizations to Contact

The editors have compiled the following list of organizations concerned with the issues debated in this book. The descriptions are derived from materials provided by the organizations. All have publications or information available for interested readers. The list was compiled on the date of publication of the present volume; the information provided here may change. Be aware that many organizations take several weeks or longer to respond to inquiries, so allow as much time as possible for the receipt of requested materials.

Advocates for Youth
2000 M St. NW, Ste. 750
Washington, DC 20036
(202) 419-3420
fax: (202) 419-1448
Website: www.advocatesforyouth.org

Advocates for Youth is an organization that works both in the United States and in developing countries with a sole focus on adolescent reproductive and sexual health. Advocates for Youth champions efforts that help young people make informed and responsible decisions about their reproductive and sexual health through its core values of "Rights, Respect, and Responsibility." Advocates for Youth publishes numerous informational essays available at its website, including "The Truth About Abstinence-Only Programs."

American Civil Liberties Union (ACLU)
125 Broad St., 18th Fl.
New York, NY 10004
(212) 549-2500
e-mail: infoaclu@aclu.org
Website: www.aclu.org

The ACLU is a national organization that works to defend Americans' civil rights as guaranteed in the US Constitution. The ACLU works in courts, legislatures, and communities to defend First Amendment rights, the right to equal protection, the right to due process, and the right to privacy. The ACLU publishes the semiannual newsletter *Civil Liberties Alert* as well as briefing papers, including the report *A Violent Education: Corporal Punishment of Children in U.S. Public Schools.*

American Library Association (ALA)
50 E. Huron
Chicago, IL 60611
(800) 545-2433
fax: (312) 440-9374
e-mail: ala@ala.org
Website: www.ala.org

The ALA is the nation's primary professional organization for librarians. The ALA provides leadership for the development, promotion, and improvement of library services and librarianship in order to enhance learning and ensure access to information for all. The ALA publishes the *Newsletter on Intellectual Freedom* online, the only journal that reports attempts to remove materials from school and library shelves across the country.

Center for Public Education
1680 Duke St.
Alexandria, VA 22314
(703) 838-6722
fax: (703) 548-5613
e-mail: centerforpubliced@nsba.org
Website: www.centerforpubliceducation.org

The Center for Public Education is a resource center set up by the National School Boards Association. The center works to provide information about public education, leading to more understanding about our schools, more community-wide involvement, and better decision making by school leaders on behalf of all students in their classrooms. Among the many publications available at the center's website is "Search and Seizure, Due Process, and Public Schools."

**The Charles Hamilton Houston Institute
for Race & Justice (CHHIRJ)**
125 Mount Auburn St., 3rd Fl.
Cambridge, MA 02138-5765
(617) 495-8285
fax: (617) 496-1406
e-mail: houstoninst@law.harvard.edu
Website: www.charleshamiltonhouston.org

The CHHIRJ honors and continues the work of one of the great civil rights lawyers of the twentieth century, Charles Hamilton Houston, who dedicated his life to using the law as a tool to reverse the unjust consequences of racial discrimination. One project of CHHIRJ, Redirecting the School to Prison Pipeline, focuses on understanding the journey for far too many children of color that begins in segregated, impoverished schools and ends in juvenile halls and adult prisons. The institute identifies and widely disseminates research-based solutions for redirecting the pipeline. Among the institute's published research is the policy brief on the topic of juvenile justice "No More Children Left Behind Bars."

Edutopia, the George Lucas Educational Foundation
PO Box 3494
San Rafael, CA 94912
(415) 662-1673
fax: (415) 662-1619
e-mail: info@edutopia.org
Website: www.edutopia.org

Edutopia, the George Lucas Educational Foundation, was created to change education by helping children become lifelong learners and develop the technical, cultural, and interpersonal skills to succeed in the twenty-first century. Edutopia works to spread the word about ideal, interactive learning environments and enable others to adapt these successes locally. Edutopia publishes the *Edutopia* magazine and the *Edutopia* video, both of which are available at its website.

National Education Association (NEA)
1201 Sixteenth St. NW
Washington, DC 20036-3290

(202) 833-4000
fax: (202) 822-7974
Website: www.nea.org

The NEA is an educator membership organization that works to advance the rights of educators and children. The NEA focuses its energy on improving the quality of teaching, increasing student achievement, and making schools safe places to learn. Among the magazines that the NEA publishes are *NEA Today* and *Thought & Action.*

National Youth Violence Prevention Resource Center (NYVPRC)
Centers for Disease Control and Prevention
1600 Clifton Rd.
Atlanta, GA 30333
(800) 232-4636
e-mail: cdcinfo@cdc.gov
We site: www.safeyouth.org

The NYVPRC was established by the Council on Youth Violence as a resource center within the Centers for Disease Control and Prevention to provide assistance to communities on effective violence prevention programs. The NYVPRC serves as a single point of access to information about youth violence and prevention strategies for the general public. Among the many publications available at its website regarding youth violence is the report "School-Associated Student Homicides: United States, 1992–2006."

Office of Juvenile Justice and Delinquency Prevention (OJJDP)
810 Seventh St. NW
Washington, DC 20531
(202) 307-5911
Website: www.ojjdp.ncjrs.org

The OJJDP, a component of the Office of Justice Programs, US Department of Justice, collaborates with professionals from diverse disciplines to improve juvenile justice policies and practices. The OJJDP accomplishes its mission by supporting states, local communities, and tribal jurisdictions in their efforts to develop and implement effective programs for juveniles. Through its Juvenile Justice Clearinghouse,

OJJDP provides access to fact sheets, summaries, and reports, including the fact sheet "Overcoming Barriers to School Reentry."

Student Drug-Testing Institute (SDTI)
8757 Georgia Ave., Ste. 1440
Silver Spring, MD 20910
(866) 956-SDTI • (866) 956-7384
e-mail: SDTI@seiservices.com
Website: http://sdti.ed.gov

The US Department of Education's Student Drug-Testing Institute provides information on many aspects of student drug-testing programs. The institute supports school efforts to implement drug-testing programs by recommending the necessary components of developing a student drug-testing program, implementing a confidential and effective program, and sustaining a program to promote drug-free students. Among the resources available at its website are publications about drug-testing programs and links to studies about drug testing.

For Further Reading

Books

Brunsma, David L., ed. *Uniforms in Public Schools: A Decade of Research and Debate.* Lanham, MD: Rowman & Littlefield Education, 2006. Multiple contributors provide empirical research and commentary on school uniform policies' effectiveness at advancing educational goals.

Cornell, Dewey G. *School Violence: Fears Versus Facts.* Mahwah, NJ: Lawrence Erlbaum, 2006. Identifies nineteen myths and misconceptions about school violence, from bullying to rampage shootings.

Dautrich, Kenneth, David A. Yalof, and Mark Hugo Lopez. *The Future of the First Amendment: The Digital Media, Civic Education, and Free Expression Rights in America's High Schools.* Lanham, MD: Rowman & Littlefield, 2008. Documents and explores the ramifications of First Amendment education and student media activities—both traditional and digital—on student support for free expression rights.

Doan, Alesha E., and Jean Calterone Williams. *The Politics of Virginity: Abstinence in Sex Education.* Westport, CT: Praeger, 2008. Argues against abstinence-only sex education programs in public schools as ineffective and damaging to women.

Lassiter, William L., and Danya C. Perry. *Preventing Violence and Crime in America's Schools: From Put-Downs to Lock-Downs.* Westport, CT: Praeger, 2009. Examines specifics relating to school violence, opportunities to prevent and intervene, and the importance of planning for a crisis.

Lawrence, Richard. *School Crime and Juvenile Justice.* New York: Oxford University Press, 2006. Examines the nature, extent, and causes of school crime and disruptive behavior, including prevention strategies.

Lieberman, Joseph A. *School Shootings: What Every Parent and Educator Needs to Know to Protect Our Children.* New York: Kensington,

2008. Offers new understanding on how many school shooters were depressed or suicidal, why it is almost always boys who commit these killings, and why so many shootings are happening.

Luker, Kristin. *When Sex Goes to School: Warring Views on Sex—and Sex Education—Since the Sixties.* New York: Norton, 2007. Explores the conflict about sex education in public school through the examination of battles over the issue in four American communities.

Meiners, Erica R. *Right to Be Hostile: Schools, Prisons, and the Making of Public Enemies.* New York: Routledge, 2007. Argues that certain educational practices disproportionately target youth of color, funneling students of color into the criminal justice system, linking schools to prisons.

Miceli, Melinda. *Standing Out, Standing Together: The Social and Political Impact of Gay-Straight Alliances.* New York: Routledge, 2005. Explores the personal and political stakes involved in the battles over gay-straight alliances in schools.

Murray, Charles. *Real Education: Four Simple Truths for Bringing America's Schools Back to Reality.* New York: Random House, 2009. Argues that school policies have focused on the unattainable goal of educating all children and contends that the educational establishment needs to focus on the gifted.

Poppendieck, Janet. *Free for All: Fixing School Food in America.* Berkeley: University of California Press, 2010. Explores the politics of food provision in public schools from multiple perspectives and concludes that healthier food is needed.

Ravitch, Diane. *The Death and Life of the Great American School System: How Testing and Choice Are Undermining Education.* New York: Basic Books, 2010. Critiques the most popular ideas for restructuring schools, including privatization, standardized testing, punitive accountability, and the multiplication of charter schools.

Thomas, R. Murray. *God in the Classroom: Religion and America's Public Schools.* Westport, CT: Praeger, 2007. Discusses the major types of conflicts over the proper role of religion in American public schools, including school prayer, holiday celebrations, and the teaching of evolution.

———. *Violence in America's Schools: Understanding, Prevention, and Responses.* Lanham, MD: Rowman & Littlefield Education, 2009. Provides a foundation for understanding why school violence occurs, how to prevent it from happening, and in what way to treat both offenders and victims after it happens.

Periodicals and Internet Sources

American Psychological Association Zero Tolerance Task Force. "Are Zero Tolerance Policies Effective in the Schools? An Evidentiary Review and Recommendations," *American Psychologist*, December 2008.

Armistead, Rhonda. "Zero Tolerance: The School Woodshed," *Education Week*, June 11, 2008.

Barbieri, Annalisa. "A Lack of Moral Fibre: School Uniforms Use Fabrics We Would Normally Avoid. Why?," *New Statesman*, July 14, 2008.

Bernard, Sara. "Moral Aptitude," *Edutopia*, August/September 2008.

Boonstra, Heather D. "The Case for a New Approach to Sex Education Mounts; Will Policymakers Heed the Message?," *Guttmacher Policy Review*, Spring 2007.

Boutelle, Marsha. "Uniforms: Are They a Good Fit?," *Education Digest*, February 2008.

Browne, Judith, and Olga Akselrod. "Bringing Common Sense Back to School Discipline," *People's World Weekly*, November 19, 2005.

Brunsma, David, interview by Samantha Stainburn. "Interview: Clothes-Minded," *Teacher*, May 1, 2005.

Campbell, Colleen Carroll. "God and the Public Schools," *Lay Witness*, September/October 2006.

Chesley, Roger. "Detector Just One Safety Tool in High Schools," *Virginian-Pilot* (Norfolk, VA), March 7, 2009.

Current Events, a Weekly Reader Publication. "Curses! Should Students Be Fined for Using Foul Language?," January 20, 2006.

Darden, Edwin C. "Search and Seizure, Due Process, and Public Schools," Center for Public Education, April 5, 2006. www.center forpubliceducation.org.

Denver Post, "School Soda Ban a Healthy Choice," December 12, 2008.

Doblin, Alfred P. "An Image of Hate Is Not Always Hate Speech," *Bergen County (NJ) Record,* September 24, 2007.

Downey, Maureen. "All Dressed Up with No Urge to Learn," *Atlanta Journal-Constitution,* December 8, 2008.

The Economist, "Badge of Honour? School Uniforms," September 26, 2009.

Fish, Stanley. "Clarence Thomas Is Right," *New York Times Online,* July 8, 2007. http://opinionator.blogs.nytimes.com/2007/07/08 /clarence-thomas-is-right.

Flesher, Jared, and Alexandra Marks. "Should Students Be Allowed to Carry Concealed Weapons?," *Christian Science Monitor,* April 18, 2007.

Gibbs, Nancy. "Birth Control for Kids?," *Time,* October 18, 2007.

Gordon, Bryony. "We Should Cut Our Ties with School Uniform," *Telegraph,* April 24, 2009.

Haynes, Charles C. "For High School Students, Free Speech Is No Joke," First Amendment Center, July 8, 2007. www.firstamend mentcenter.org.

Hendricks, Mike. "Too Much Junk Food in Our Schools," *Kansas City (MO) Star,* August 14, 2007.

Herbert, Bob. "Poisonous Police Behavior," *New York Times,* June 2, 2007.

Hess, Frederick M. "Do Student Rights Interfere with Teaching and Learning in Public Schools?," *CQ Researcher,* June 1, 2009.

Hillenbrand, Shawn. "School Uniforms Are Inconvenient, Unnecessary," *Evansville (IN) Courier & Press,* February 28, 2010. www.courierpress.com.

Howard, Philip K. "Class War," *Wall Street Journal,* May 24, 2005.

Junior Scholastic, "Should Kids Be Required to Wear School Uniforms?," September 4, 2006.

Kapner, Suzanne. "Dress Code," *Fortune,* August 31, 2009.

Kern, Jennifer. "Random Student Drug Testing Is Not the Answer," *Huffington Post,* May 7, 2008. www.huffingtonpost.com.

Kliff, Sarah. "The New Abstinence-Education Study Is Good News. So Why Are Liberals Freaking Out?," *Newsweek*, February 3, 2010.

Marshall, Jennifer A. "Empower Women: Teach Abstinence," Heritage Foundation, February 8, 2010.

McKeon, Brigid. "Effective Sex Education," Advocates for Youth, 2006. www.advocatesforyouth.org.

New York Times, "Abstinence Education Done Right," February 7, 2010.

Orlando Sentinel, "Give School Uniforms a Look," September 4, 2009.

Page, Jeffrey. "A Way to Help Make Our Schools Safer," *Bergen County (NJ) Record*, October 31, 2006.

Perry, Andre. "Why Schools Must Teach Morality," *Times-Picayune* (New Orleans, LA), January 31, 2009.

Rosenbaum, Marsha. "Student Drug Testing Is No 'Silver Bullet,'" *San Diego Union-Tribune*, February 22, 2006.

Sklar, Brian. "How Much Do Christians Have to Give Up?," *Kitchner (ON) Record,*, December 4, 2009.

Tanner, Julian. "Making Schools Safer? The Unintended Consequences of Good Intentions," *Education Canada*, 2009.

Tirozzi, Gerald N. "Another View: Err on the Side of Safety," *USA Today*, November 11, 2009.

USA Today, "Our View on Freedom of Expression: Protect Student Speech—Even 'Unwise' Bong Banner," March 21, 2007.

Wilkinson, Will. "The Real School Indoctrination Scandal," *The Week*, September 16, 2009.

Yassky, David. "Why Not Detention?," *New York Sun*, November 21, 2007.

Websites

Freedom Forum (www.freedomforum.org). This website of the Freedom Forum, a nonpartisan foundation dedicated to free press, free speech, and free spirit for all people, contains information about the First Amendment and freedom of expression.

National Center for Education Statistics (http://nces.ed.gov). This website provides data related to education, including statistics on the extent of school policies such as drug testing and school safety initiatives.

Student Drug Testing Coalition (www.studentdrugtesting.org). This website provides technical resources, materials, and information about student drug testing programs.

Index

Picture Credits